Extreme
Love

The GREATEST
COMMANDMENT

LifeWay Press®
Nashville, Tennessee

ISBN: 0-6331-9383-6
This book is a resource in the Personal Life category of the Christian Growth Study Plan.
CG-1026
Dewey Decimal Classification Number: 248.84
Subject Heading: CHRISTIAN LIFE \ LOVE \ BIBLE. N.T. MARK 12:28-31—STUDY

Unless otherwise noted, all Scripture quotations are taken from the Holman Christian Standard Bible®
Copyright © 1999, 2000, 2002, 2004 by Holman Bible Publishers. Used by permission.
Scripture quotations marked (AMP) are taken from The Amplified® Bible, copyright © 1954,1958, 1962, 1964, 1965, 1987 by The Lockman Foundation. Used by permission. *(www.lockman.org)*
Scripture quotations marked (The Message) are taken from The Message by Eugene H. Peterson, copyright (c) 1993, 1994, 1995, 1996, 2000, 2001, 2002. Used by permission of NavPress Publishing Group. All rights reserved.
Scripture quotations marked (NASB)® are taken from the New American Standard Bible®, Copyright © 1960, 1962, 1963, 1968, 1971, 1972, 1973, 1975, 1977, 1995 by The Lockman Foundation. Used by permission. *(www.lockman.org)*
Scripture quotations marked (NIV) are from the Holy Bible, New International Version, copyright © 1973, 1978, 1984 by International Bible Society.
Scripture quotations marked (NLT) are taken from the Holy Bible, New Living Translation, copyright © 1996. Used by permission of Tyndale House Publishers, Inc., Wheaton, IL 60189 USA. All rights reserved.

We believe the Bible has God for its author; salvation for its end; and truth, without any mixture of error, for its matter and that all Scripture is totally true and trustworthy. The 2000 statement of *The Baptist Faith and Message* is our doctrinal guideline.

To order additional copies of this resource: WRITE LifeWay Church Resources Customer Service; One LifeWay Plaza; Nashville, TN 37234-0113; FAX order to (615) 251-5933; PHONE (800) 458-2772; E-MAIL to *customerservice@lifeway.com;* ORDER ONLINE at *www.lifeway.com;* or VISIT the LifeWay Christian Store serving you.

Printed in the United States of America
Leadership and Adult Publishing
LifeWay Church Resources
One LifeWay Plaza
Nashville, Tennessee 37234-0175

Contents

Introduction

Every adventure begins with a choice. You can choose to live your life in isolation or in relationship. Jesus' Greatest Commandment calls us to live in relationship—in relationship with God and in relationship with one another. Jesus said that two things are important—loving God and loving others. This is the Greatest Commandment.

> One of the scribes approached. When he heard them debating and saw that Jesus answered them well, he asked Him, "Which commandment is the most important of all?"
> "This is the most important," Jesus answered:
> Hear, O Israel! The Lord our God is one Lord. And you shall love the Lord your God with all your heart, with all your soul, with all your mind, and with all your strength.
> "The second is: 'You shall love your neighbor as yourself.' There is no other commandment greater than these" (Mark 12:28-31).

That's Extreme Love!

Our adventure is about to begin. Will you join us?

Total Experience

This study focuses on the Greatest Commandment. The goal is to allow you to examine Jesus' command from several different angles and to gain new insights from each. The purpose is not to segment the individual parts of this passage—heart, soul, mind, strength—but to see it in new ways so that you can apply these truths to your own life.

Small-Group Sessions

This study contains seven sessions. Each session is designed so that all who want to participate should be welcome, regardless of whether they have participated in previous sessions or can commit to attending all the sessions.

One of the benefits of this combination Bible study and daily devotional experience is to join other adults in your congregation in focusing entirely on one primary concept for 40 days of Bible study. Such a focus can help you gain new insights from the Bible and strengthen your own personal relationship with Jesus Christ.

The first session is an introductory session. It does not count as one of the 40 days. Each subsequent small-group session counts as one of the 40 days.

Each small-group session is divided into sections to help you move through the lesson. At or near the beginning you will find a story that applies the Scripture to be studied in that session.

In addition to the introductory narrative, each small-group session has six parts. Each part has an icon.

Share uses questions to help group members interact with and learn about one another.

Declare contains questions that guide group members to examine Bible passages.

Dare challenges group members to apply the biblical truths to their lives.

Care suggests ways for group members to show love and concern for one another and for people outside their small group.

Prayer directs participants to communicate with God about a need revealed in this session.

Aware contains background information to assist group members in understanding the meaning of the Scripture.

Sermon Notes

If your church's worship services are also focusing on The Greatest Commandment, you may want to take notes on the sermons to enhance your learning experience. Sermon Notes pages are provided for this purpose.

Devotionals

Following the small-group sessions are daily devotionals. The devotionals reinforce the truths discovered in the sessions. Each devotional ends with a challenge for the reader. It can be identified by one of the icons found in the small-group sessions.

The Greatest Commandment

*God is love, and He wants you
to love Him completely.*

I hadn't been back to Stuart's Lake since I was 10 years old, but I felt compelled to drive down the gravel road that spring afternoon. I arrived shortly before sunset the day before my father's funeral. The lake seemed smaller than I remembered, but just as magical, surrounded by pines that cast shadows in the late afternoon. Dad and I used to go there to fish, to play, and to talk about everything and nothing in particular.

I learned to skip rocks there, too. I loved watching the ripples move across the water until they faded from sight. Now, as I tossed a rock into the lake, I saw my distorted reflection and realized that, instead of gentle ripples, my life felt like it was caught in the chaos of shock waves following an earthquake.

When I was a child, this was the center of my universe. When I was here, I felt my father's love. Now he was gone, and my world felt out of control.

SHARE

1. Recall a song with the word *love* that was popular when you were a teenager.
2. Recall a hymn or chorus that uses the word *love*.
3. Compare and contrast the meaning of *love* in these two songs.

DECLARE

1. **Read Mark 12:28-31:**

> One of the scribes approached. When he heard them debating and saw that Jesus answered them well, he asked Him, "Which commandment is the most important of all?"

"This is the most important," Jesus answered:

> Hear, O Israel! The Lord our God is one Lord. And you shall love the Lord your God with all your heart, with all your soul, with all your mind, and with all your strength.

"The second is: 'You shall love your neighbor as yourself.' There is no other commandment greater than these."

- What did the scribe ask Jesus?

- What might have prompted him to ask this question?

- What do you think "the Lord our God is one Lord" means?

- Read Exodus 20:2:
    "I am the Lord your God, who brought you out of Egypt, out of the land of slavery" (NIV).

    This declaration introduces the Ten Commandments. What is the significance of God's making this statement before giving the Ten Commandments?

- In Mark 12:30-31, what did Jesus say is the most important commandment?

- What is the second part of this commandment?

- The Ten Commandments are listed below. Place a **1** in the space beside the commandment if it relates to the first part of the Greatest Commandment and a **2** in the space if it relates to the second part.
    ____ 1. Do not have other gods besides Me.
    ____ 2. Do not make an idol for yourself, whether in the shape of anything in the heavens above or on the earth below or in the waters under the earth.
    ____ 3. Do not misuse the name of the LORD your God, because the LORD will punish anyone who misuses His name.
    ____ 4. Remember to dedicate the Sabbath day: You are to labor six days and do all your work, but the seventh day is a Sabbath to the LORD your God.
    ____ 5. Honor your father and your mother so that you may have a long life in the land that the LORD your God is giving you.
    ____ 6. Do not murder.
    ____ 7. Do not commit adultery.
    ____ 8. Do not steal.
    ____ 9. Do not give false testimony against your neighbor.
    ____ 10. Do not covet your neighbor's house. Do not covet your neighbor's wife, his male or female slave, his ox or donkey, or anything that belongs to your neighbor.

2. **Read Matthew 22:34-40:**
    When the Pharisees heard that He had silenced the Sadducees, they
    came together in the same place. And one of them, an expert in the law,
    asked a question to test Him: "Teacher, which commandment in the law
    is the greatest?"
        He said to him, "You shall love the Lord your God with all your heart, with
    all your soul, and with all your mind. This is the greatest and most important
    commandment. The second is like it: You shall love your neighbor as yourself.
    All the Law and the Prophets depend on these two commandments."

- "The Law and the Prophets" represents a large portion of the Old Testament. The Law
  is the first five books, which contains the Ten Commandments and other Jewish laws
  and rules. What do you think the last sentence of Matthew 22:34-40 means?

3. **Read 1 John 4:7-11:**
    Dear friends, let us love one another, because love is from God, and everyone
    who loves has been born of God and knows God. The one who does not love
    does not know God, because God is love. God's love was revealed among us
    in this way: God sent His One and Only Son into the world so that we might
    live through Him. Love consists in this: not that we loved God, but that He
    loved us and sent His Son to be the propitiation for our sins. Dear friends,
    if God loved us in this way, we also must love one another.

- In what way does Jesus show God's love?

- In both the Greatest Commandment and 1 John, what are we commanded to do?

DARE

1. What does your world revolve around?

2. What would those closest to you say is the center of your universe?

3. When something affects your center, what are the ripple effects?

4. How would you be different if God were the center of your universe?

CARE

1. How would those closest to you know if God became more the center of your universe?

2. When God is the center of your universe, how do ripples in your world affect you and the people around you?

PRAYER

Ask God to reveal the true center of your universe and to help you let Him become that center in you.

AWARE

Greatest Commandment—Jesus' response to the scribe, giving the Greatest Commandment, is a quotation from Deuteronomy 6:4-5, the first part of the Shema (see explanation below). Matthew and Luke do not include the sentence, "Hear, O Israel: the LORD our God, the LORD is one" (NIV). But it is a crucial sentence because the obligation to love God is based on His oneness. Because He is one, love for Him must be undivided. The piling up of the terms *heart, soul, mind,* and *strength* is not intended to designate the component parts of human nature but to reinforce the concept of loving God with one's entire being.

The second quotation is from Leviticus 19:18. In the first part of that verse *neighbor* is defined as "one of your people," an Israelite. Leviticus 19:33-34 extends the love command to resident aliens. One of the most significant elements in the teaching of Jesus was to redefine *neighbor* to mean everybody, including the hated Samaritans and Gentiles.

Jesus' teaching also brought together the commands to love God and to love people. Even if a few others before or during the time of Jesus saw the interrelationship of the commands to love God and others, no one else put such great emphasis on the combination and made it essential. Jesus showed that it was really impossible to love God without loving neighbors. Love for God is expressed by loving others.

Shema—From the Hebrew word meaning "to hear," it was the basic statement of Jewish law. For the people of God, it became a confession of faith by which they acknowledged the one true God and His commandments. When Jesus was asked about the "greatest commandment," He answered by quoting the Shema, Deuteronomy 6:4-5. This was a familiar passage to the Jews, including Jesus, one they recited daily.

One God or many gods?—One of the great distinctives of Judeo-Christian religion is monotheism, the recognition and reverence of only one God. By contrast, pagan religions of the biblical world were polytheistic, worshiping many gods. The fertility aspect of the Canaanite gods was an inviting snare to the Israelites. New to farming, and having just settled in Canaan after a generation of nomadic life in the desert, the Israelites were particularly tempted to serve the gods said to control the fertility of the land.

The pagan gods of the New Testament world were the deities of the Greco-Roman pantheon and certain Eastern gods whose myths gave rise to the mystery religions. Idols were physical or material images or forms representing a reality or being considered divine and thus an object of worship. The ancient Hebrews lived in a world filled with idols.

Scribe—A person trained in writing skills in order to record events and decisions. During the exile in Babylon, educated scribes became the experts in God's written Word—copying, preserving, and teaching it. By New Testament times a professional group of scribes had developed. Most were Pharisees. They interpreted the Law, taught it to disciples, and were experts in cases where people were accused of breaking the Law of Moses. They led in plans to kill Jesus and heard His stern rebuke.

Sermon Notes / **The Greatest Commandment**

Scripture Text

Main Points
1.

2.

3.

Meaningful Illustrations

Personal Application

DAY 1 — God Is Love

God is love. If you miss out on God, you miss out on love. And, as a simple matter of fact, most do. Why? There are billions of people, each with a different reason. But the fact remains that if we are to experience a life of truth, passion, and fulfillment, we must first have an encounter with God and the truth about God. The Bible says, "God is love. When we take up permanent residence in a life of love, we live in God and God lives in us" (1 John 4:16, *The Message*). Let those words go down deeper than Sunday songs and bumper-sticker slogans.

God is love.

He is not another impossible task. He's not a cosmic commando, ready to fire spiritual missiles at you every time you mess up. God is not the enemy. He loves you. He is for you. And if you have never reached out to Him, be assured that He's reaching out to you.

Jesus loves you unconditionally, which is hard to accept because we live in a world of terms, fine print, loopholes, and exceptions. He is offering you the greatest gift you could ever receive. He loves you so much that He ignored the consequences in order to bring you into a right relationship with God.

What's the catch? The catch is that you can't earn your way into an eternal relationship with Him. He simply asks you to drop all your tools, coping mechanisms, and survival strategies and come.

That's extreme love! Its DNA finds its origin in God. John, one of Jesus' closest companions, said, "This is real love. It is not that we loved God, but that he loved us and sent his Son as a sacrifice to take away our sins" (1 John 4:10, NLT).

You may have lived your entire life going to church. Or you might never have been to a church. That's OK, too. For these 40 days, look squarely at the truth about God and His extreme love. His love can change the very nature and direction of your life—

No matter who you are.

No matter where you've been.

No matter what you've done.

Period.

DARE

Write down three main obstacles that inhibit you from experiencing the extreme love of God.

The Main Thing

God wants you. He desires a unique, true, and intimate relationship with you right now and forever more. The one elite, distinctive, and important declaration in the Old Testament about this relationship is called the Shema. It's the confession of faith that is said by devout Jews at least twice a day, morning and evening.

> Hear, O Israel: The LORD our God, the LORD is one. Love the LORD your God with all your heart and with all your soul and with all your strength. These commandments that I give you today are to be upon your hearts. Impress them on your children. Talk about them when you sit at home and when you walk along the road, when you lie down and when you get up. Tie them as symbols on your hands and bind them on your foreheads. Write them on the doorframes of your houses and on your gates (Deut. 6:4-9, NIV).

In a culture that said "the more gods the better," the one true God said, "Wrong. There's only one." The declaration is that God is not a graven image or a list of rules, despite the legalistic tendencies of religious people. The main thing is that there is one God, and He desires a love relationship with you.

This relationship should be so vibrant and alive that it becomes the focus of dinner-table talk and long-walk conversations. It should be job one for a parent. We should remind ourselves about this love agreement with symbols, declarations, and prayers. God says loudly, "Listen! This is the one thing I want really want you to get. I am the One, and I want your love."

Let's fast forward a few thousand years and realize that this same God is still here, and He's still reaching. The world is still serving a multitude of graven images and gods. Our culture flits from one god to the next through media circuses, satellite events, magic pills, and tantalizing scenarios. And God still calls out to the world.

I
am
One.

SHARE

This week talk about God with the people closest to you as you work, walk, play, and worship.

DAY 3 God's Love Came First

God's love doesn't begin with us. Listen to Jesus' friend John once more: "We love because he first loved us" (1 John 4:19, NIV). God was the first to love. His love took the initiative before you drew your first breath. He loved you before you did anything at all.

Jesus loved. That small subject-verb sentence says it all! That was the major message when He walked the earth. "Having loved His own who were in the world, He loved them to the end" (John 13:1, NASB).

God's love is alive and well. His love isn't just a principle. It's a verb. He's still entering homes where we wouldn't dare go. He's still touching the diseased world in places we choose to quarantine. He's still calming storms, washing feet, and feeding His children.

Yes, His love invades us, surrounds us, and extends far beyond our greatest reach. The power of God's love is healing the hopeless, calling believers, installing His Spirit, directing His servants, correcting the liars, reconciling the schisms, rejuvenating the weary, reforming the church, transforming our identity, rectifying relationships, appointing ambassadors, redeeming the debt, reclaiming the world, and proclaiming freedom. His love is not only present; it is working!

> What marvelous love the Father has extended to us! Just look at it—we're called children of God! That's who we really are. But that's also why the world doesn't recognize us or take us seriously, because it has no idea who he is or what he's up to (1 John 3:1, *The Message*).

His love keeps seeking and reaching and encompassing. And nothing can stop it. He is the original artisan of love!

PRAYER

Lord, today I celebrate Your love. You reached out Your hand to me when I was without hope. In the past I've closed my hands into a fist and defiantly said no to You, but You loved me anyway. Your hands sought to reconcile and not to exclude. I want my hands to be like Yours: Hands that seek to heal and not to strike. Hands to build and not to destroy. Hands that are open. Hands that are clean and a heart that is pure. I worship You. A living, resurrected, and reigning Lord. As you extend Your hands to us, thank You, Father.

Who's Your Favorite?

Her small hands held the glue stick as she dotted the construction paper. Her Sunday School masterpiece slowly came together. All the other children had finished and happily retreated to the swings and slides before worship. But Kellie continued. "It's my family," she said to me. "My mom, dad, brother, sister, grandmom, my kitty, and me." Her attention to detail amazed me. "And do you know who my favorite one is?" she asked, smiling as her eyes scanned the project. I didn't know exactly what to say, but she really seemed intent on an answer.

"Let me guess. . . . Your Mom?"

"No. My favorite one is me!" She chirped happily.

She hadn't learned the skill of false humility. But truth be told, God sees in our actions, attitudes, and reactions who holds the place of "favorite" in the picture of our lives.

The Bible urges the follower of God, "Don't be selfish; don't live to make a good impression on others" (Phil. 2:3, NLT).

Jesus takes this philosophy and shifts it into high gear when He tells us to love—not *tolerate* but *love* our enemies. Just read His revolutionary words:

> Do you think you deserve credit merely for loving those who love you? Even the sinners do that! And if you do good only to those who do good to you, is that so wonderful? Even sinners do that much! And if you lend money only to those who can repay you, what good is that? Even sinners will lend to their own kind for a full return. Love your enemies! Do good to them! Lend to them! And don't be concerned that they might not repay. Then your reward from heaven will be very great, and you will truly be acting as children of the Most High, for he is kind to the unthankful and to those who are wicked. You must be compassionate, just as your Father is compassionate (Luke 6:32-36, NLT).

CARE

Today honor God's love for you by finding a way to express love to someone you know who is difficult to love.

DAY 5 — What's Love Got to Do with It?

A popular song in the 1980s asked a question that deserves an answer: "What's love got to do with it?" For the Christian the answer is, "Absolutely everything." Love is the root command of the entire Bible. It is the central characteristic of God. And it must be yours if you are to love others as Jesus loves you.

The Bible says:

> Think of yourselves the way Christ Jesus thought of himself. He had equal status with God but didn't think so much of himself that he had to cling to the advantages of that status no matter what. Not at all. When the time came, he set aside the privileges of deity and took on the status of a slave, became human! Having become human, he stayed human. It was an incredibly humbling process. He didn't claim special privileges. Instead, he lived a selfless, obedient life and then died a selfless, obedient death—and the worst kind of death at that: a crucifixion (Phil. 2:5-8, *The Message*).

Jesus said:

> Just as the Father has loved Me, I also have loved you. Remain in My love. If you keep My commandments, you will remain in My love, just as I have kept My Father's commandments and remain in His love (John 15:9-10).

If a member of the press had been there, perhaps he would have raised his hand and asked that age-old question, "Why?" Lucky for us, in the next verse Jesus gives us the answer, and the answer is thrilling.

> "I have told you this so that you will be filled with my joy. Yes, your joy will overflow!" (John 15:11, NLT).

Love and real joy are inseparable. That's what love has to do with it.

PRAYER

Lord, show me Your great, unconditional, revolutionary, overflowing love. In the name of Jesus, the greatest Lover of them all. Amen.

It's a Love Story

The story of the world and everything in it is a love story. A small story tucked away in the middle of the Bible speaks volumes about God's love for us. It's the love story of a preacher and his wife, a prostitute. Hard to believe? Read on.

Hosea loved his wife with an unconditional love. The scoffers laughed: "Look at Hosea! He's at it again, looking for his beloved wife."

Hosea would search and eventually find her in the red-light district. Despite her lying, despite her adultery, Hosea loved his bride. Despite her cruelty, despite her sin, Hosea loved his wife.

At the apex of this romantic catastrophe, Hosea again searched the inner city for his wife. And off in the distance he saw her. She was an ugly sight. Bruised, beaten, naked, humiliated, destroyed. She had nothing. Hosea went back to their house and frantically gathered up all their possessions—their money, their food, everything of value. He ran to the auction block, and as the bidding began, Hosea cried out, "I'll give everything I have!"

The crowd slowly parted as he covered her trembling, humiliated body. He picked her up, this broken woman who had been enslaved. He picked her up and carried her home.

Paid in full.

And there was a time when God looked down on the auction block of the world and saw you and me. An ugly sight. Bruised, beaten, naked, humiliated, destroyed, enslaved to sin. We had nothing. But God gave everything that He had, His beloved Son, to pay the price for our sin.

It's the kind of love that knows no boundaries. A righteous thing. A tender thing. A strong thing. Amazing. It is sweet. It is grace. Greater love? There is none. It is found in God alone.

> God demonstrates his own love for us in this: While we were still sinners,
> Christ died for us (Rom. 5:8, NIV).

Have you accepted His offer? If you are ready to enter into this incredible relationship, pray this prayer right now.

PRAYER

Lord Jesus, I am tired of trying to live my life by myself. I'm tired of trying to measure up to worldly standards and expectations. I'm stopping all my self-saving attempts because I realize that my only hope is You. I believe in You. I turn away from living outside Your grace. I accept Your forgiveness and eternal life. I accept Your invitation to join You and become a part of Your family here on earth. In your name I pray. Amen.

7 DAY All Your Heart

God wants an intimate relationship with you that is real and personal.

SHARE
What makes you glad?

What makes you sad?

What makes you mad?

When we gaze upon the gravestone of a young friend, a spouse, or a brother, we encounter a common question: Where were you, Lord? Martha, one of Jesus' closest friends, asked that same question shortly after the death of her brother, Lazarus. "Lord, if You had been here, my brother wouldn't have died" (John 11:21).

Rolled into this story are the deepest questions we will ever ask about the will and nature of God. But perhaps the greatest truth of this story is found in the shortest verse in the Bible. We understand that Jesus had power over death. We know that God's timing is not always our timing. We can grasp the inescapable fact that Jesus achieved the unspeakable to signify the glory of His Father. But absorb this one fact. "Jesus wept" (John 11:35).

Why does this verse connect with us? Why did Jesus weep? Jesus wept because He has always had a heart for hurting people. Hearing the cries of those He loved connected with Him emotionally. As a father weeps for his brokenhearted daughter, Jesus weeps for us.

Know this. While our Lord is powerful beyond measure, He is also a God who desires an intimate, emotional relationship with those who call Him Lord.

DECLARE

1. Read 1 Samuel 13:14:

> The LORD has sought out a man after his own heart and appointed him leader of his people (NIV).

• What does it mean to have a heart like God's?

• What character traits do you associate with having a heart like God's?

2. Read 1 Samuel 16:7:

> But the LORD said to Samuel, "Do not consider his appearance or his height, for I have rejected him. The LORD does not look at the things man looks at. Man looks at the outward appearance, but the LORD looks at the heart" (NIV).

• What does it mean for God to look on the heart?

• If God were looking at your heart right now, what would He see? Write it here.

3. Read 1 Samuel 16:11-13:

> So he asked Jesse, "Are these all the sons you have?"
> "There is still the youngest," Jesse answered, "but he is tending the sheep." Samuel said, "Send for him; we will not sit down until he arrives."
> So he sent and had him brought in. He was ruddy, with a fine appearance and handsome features.
> Then the LORD said, "Rise and anoint him; he is the one."
> So Samuel took the horn of oil and anointed him in the presence of his brothers, and from that day on the Spirit of the LORD came upon David in power. Samuel then went to Ramah (NIV).

Read Acts 13:21-23:

> "Then they asked for a king, so God gave them Saul the son of Kish, a man of the tribe of Benjamin, for 40 years. After removing him, He raised up David as their king, of whom He testified: 'I have found David the son of Jesse, a man after My heart, who will carry out all My will.'
> "From this man's descendants, according to the promise, God brought the Savior, Jesus, to Israel."

- God led Samuel to anoint David to be the next king of Israel. In what ways did David have a heart like God's?

4. Read Luke 2:19:

    But Mary was treasuring up all these things in her heart and meditating on them.

- Based on Luke 1–2, recall recent events in Mary's life. At that moment what do you think she treasured in her heart?

5. Read Luke 2:41-52:

    Every year His parents traveled to Jerusalem for the Passover Festival. When He was 12 years old, they went up according to the custom of the festival. After those days were over, as they were returning, the boy Jesus stayed behind in Jerusalem, but His parents did not know it. Assuming He was in the traveling party, they went a day's journey. Then they began looking for Him among their relatives and friends. When they did not find Him, they returned to Jerusalem to search for Him. After three days, they found Him in the temple complex sitting among the teachers, listening to them and asking them questions. And all those who heard Him were astounded at His understanding and His answers. When His parents saw Him, they were astonished, and His mother said to Him, "Son, why have You treated us like this? Your father and I have been anxiously searching for You."

    "Why were you searching for Me?" He asked them. "Didn't you know that I must be involved in My Father's interests?" But they did not understand what He said to them.

    Then He went down with them and came to Nazareth, and was obedient to them. His mother kept all these things in her heart. And Jesus increased in wisdom and stature, and in favor with God and with people.

- Jesus is now 12 years old. In what ways was Jesus growing?

- From this experience what does Mary add to the treasures in her heart?

- In what ways does his early development reflect the Greatest Commandment?

7. Read Matthew 6:21:

    For where your treasure is, there your heart will be also.

- What do you treasure in *your* heart?

DARE

If you had a heart like Jesus, what would make you glad?

What would make you mad?

What would make you sad?

CARE
Read Galatians 6:2,9:

> Carry one another's burdens; in this way you will fulfill the law of Christ. . . . So we must not get tired of doing good, for we will reap at the proper time if we don't give up.

- A part of loving God with all your heart is caring for one another. Who needs your heartfelt ministry this week?

PRAYER
Read Philippians 4:6-7:

> Don't worry about anything, but in everything, through prayer and petition with thanksgiving, let your requests be made known to God. And the peace of God, which surpasses every thought, will guard your hearts and your minds in Christ Jesus.

- What are you worried about right now. Write it here. Give it to God in prayer.

May the peace of God guard your heart.

AWARE

Heart—The center of the physical, mental, and spiritual life of humans. The word *heart* refers to the physical organ and is considered to be the center of the physical life. As the center of physical life, the heart came to stand for the person as a whole. It became the focus for all the vital functions of the body, including both intellectual and spiritual life.

The heart and the intellect are closely connected, the heart being the seat of a person's intelligence. The heart is also connected with thinking. To ponder something in one's heart is to consider it carefully. "To set one's heart on" means to give attention to something or to worry about it. Closely related to the mind are acts of will, resulting from a conscious or deliberate decision. Connected to the will are human wishes and desires.

The heart is also connected to feelings and affections. Emotions such as joy originate in the heart. Other emotions ascribed to the heart, especially in the Old Testament, include fear, sorrow, jealousy, love, and hate.

Scripture also speaks of heart as the center of moral and spiritual life. The conscience, for example, is associated with the heart. Sometimes the heart is used to represent a person's true nature or character. This true nature is contrasted with the outward appearance. Depravity is also said to issue from the heart. Jesus said that out of the heart come evil thoughts, murder, adultery, fornication, theft, false witness, and slander. In other words, defilement comes from within rather than from without.

Because the heart is at the root of the problem, this is the place where God does His work. In addition to being the place where the natural laws of God are written, the heart is the place of renewal. Before Saul became king, God gave him a new heart. Paul said that a person must believe in his heart to be saved. The heart is the dwelling place of God.

Saul—Saul was the first king of a united Israel, a tall and handsome man from the tribe of Benjamin (1 Sam. 9:1-2,21). Chosen by God and secretly anointed by Samuel (10:1), Saul was later selected publicly by lot. Saul's reign is generally dated about 1020–1000 B.C. Saul disobeyed God, and God rejected him as king.

David—David, the second king of Israel, was the first king to unite Israel and Judah and the first to receive the promise of a royal messiah in his line. He ruled from about 1005 to 965 B.C. during the Golden Age of Israel. He established Jerusalem as the capital city. Although God did not allow him to build the temple there, he supplied the resources for his son Solomon to build the temple when he became king. Although David sinned in his relationship with Bathsheba, David was called "a man after God's own heart." He wrote many of the psalms, included Psalm 51, a psalm of repentance.

Scripture Text

Main Points
1.

2.

3.

Meaningful Illustrations

Personal Application

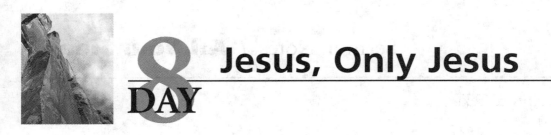

DAY 8 — Jesus, Only Jesus

What is your greatest secret longing? Is it to know the heart of God? To know Jesus is to know the heart of God. Isn't that what you want? Maybe you've tried to fill that deep sense of longing in other ways. You wouldn't be the first. The Israelites tried to create a relationship with God their own way, too. But they failed miserably.

> "We long for light but sink into darkness, long for brightness but stumble through the night. Like the blind, we inch along a wall, groping eyeless in the dark. We shuffle our way in broad daylight, like the dead, but somehow walking" (Isa. 59:9-10, *The Message*).

You, too, might feel like you are blindly groping your way to God. But it doesn't have to be that way. The simple reality is that you come to know God only as you enter into a personal relationship with His Son, Jesus Christ. Looking any other direction—stumbling in the dark down any other path—is only to limit what it means to know God. Jesus said, "I am the Road, also the Truth, also the Life. No one gets to the Father apart from me" (John 14:6, *The Message*).

To love God with all your heart is to realize that Jesus is the only way. It's not a politically correct statement, but it is truth. Want to reach the heart of God? Jesus. Only Jesus. Want contentment and peace? Jesus. Only Jesus. Want to live forever, go to heaven, and take as many of your friends with you as you can? Jesus. Only Jesus.

PRAYER

Lord, I am making a decisive dedication of my life to You! I give You my whole heart. Because Your love for me was a choice, I, too, make the choice to love You. I was bought with a price, and I am a child of God. Because of whose I am, I know that my life has purpose and significance. This life is not a meaningless journey. When I give my heart to You, I have great purpose and significance. I love You, Lord. Amen.

A Heart Exam

God is interested in what's going on inside you. What is the condition of your heart at this point in your journey toward eternity? If you are unsure, allow God right now to speak to You. He will. Just shut everything else off and listen.

Jesus said to the rigid, rules-before-relationship people, "You like to look good in public, but God knows your evil hearts. What this world honors is an abomination in the sight of God" (Luke 16:15, NLT). God isn't impressed with exteriors. When God wanted to find just the right man for the job of leading His chosen people, He said, "The LORD does not look at the things man looks at. Man looks at the outward appearance, but the LORD looks at the heart" (1 Sam. 16:7, NIV).

God desires from you, more than anything else, a heart that is pure. An ancient song echoes this truth: "Who can climb Mount God? Who can scale the holy north-face? Only the clean-handed, only the pure-hearted" (Ps. 24:3-4, *The Message*).

Perhaps you have been a part of God's family for years, but cynicism and bitterness have stolen your passion for God. You are not alone. Jesus hasn't lost His passion for you. You've worked for Him. You've callused your hands for His approval. Stop for a moment. Jesus says to you, "You have patiently suffered for me without quitting. But I have this complaint against you. You don't love me or each other as you did at first! Look how far you have fallen from your first love!" (Rev. 2:3-5, NLT).

Could it be that you've become wishy-washy or cynical about your spiritual world? Jesus has a warning. "I know you inside and out, and find little to my liking. You're not cold, you're not hot—far better to be either cold or hot! You're stale. You're stagnant. You make me want to vomit. You brag, 'I'm rich, I've got it made, I need nothing from anyone,' oblivious that in fact you're a pitiful, blind beggar, threadbare and homeless" (Rev. 3:15-17, *The Message*).

Jesus wants you to stop doing and start becoming. Jesus doesn't call you to be somebody. He has called you to contain Someone. He's not impressed with your tricks, and He doesn't simply want to be a conduit of treats. Take a minute and examine your heart. Say to God, "Help me understand the meaning of your commandments, and I will meditate on your wonderful miracles" (Ps. 119: 27, NLT).

PRAYER

Lord, I want to worship and adore You above all else. You are a great God, a merciful God, a mighty God. Mighty is Your name. Your peace transcends all understanding. You became sin for me so that I could be considered righteous. Savior is Your name! You forgave all my sins. Holy is Your name! You make bitter experiences sweet. When I am weak, You are strong on my behalf. Redeemer is Your name. Hallelujah! Amen.

DAY 10 Rebelling, Drifting, or Resting

Several men were preparing to canoe down a river. "You'll navigate the water just fine if you remember two things," said their guide. "First, the river can easily lull you into a false sense of security, so pay attention at all times. And second, make sure you veer to the right when the river forks. The left fork is dangerous white water that is too powerful for canoes. Don't be a daredevil. It'll cost you."

A few miles down the river, one man relaxed. The water was calm, so he closed his eyes. The next thing he knew, his canoe was stuck firmly on a sandbar. Try as he might, he couldn't dislodge it.

Another man on the same excursion decided to prove his whitewater skills by ignoring the "left fork" warning. Moments later he hit churning whitewater that sucked him and his canoe under an outcrop of jagged rocks. He clawed his way to the surface only to have the churning water throw him into another pile of rocks, where he hung on, bruised and bleeding, in the ice cold water until rescue workers found him hours later.

Drifting and rebelling are two dangerous enemies of the heart. The writer of the Book of Hebrews underscores today's message to you.

> It's crucial that we keep a firm grip on what we've heard so that we don't drift off. If the old message delivered by the angels was valid and nobody got away with anything, do you think we can risk neglecting this latest message, this magnificent salvation? First of all, it was delivered in person by the Master, then accurately passed on to us by those who heard it from him (Heb. 2:1-3, *The Message*).

How's your grip on the message of Jesus?

And of rebellion the Bible states:

> Today you must listen to his voice. Don't harden your hearts against Him [God] as Israel did when they rebelled, when they tested God's patience in the wilderness. There your ancestors tried my patience, even though they saw my miracles for forty years. So I was angry with them, and I said, "Their hearts always turn away from me. They refuse to do what I tell them." So in my anger I made a vow: "They will never enter my place of rest" (Heb. 3:7-11, NLT).

AWARE

Do you wish to live in a state of rebellious exhaustion, pointless drifting, or restful reliance?

Where Your Treasure Is

We don't know a great deal about Mary, the mother of Jesus. We do know that God changed her life from the moment the angel Gabriel visited her. She held the Son of God that night. Jesus was His name. It was a holy night. God's glory came to earth and wrote a love letter in flesh and bone—*Jesus.*

Luke's Gospel tells us that Mary treasured the details of Jesus' birth and held them in her heart. She could have griped about the travel arrangements, the lack of planning, the constant need to improvise. But Mary—in a barn full of visiting animals, horses, mules, stray dogs, camels, splinters, and hay—kept all these things and treasured them in her heart (see Luke 2:19).

That night she had to contend with Joseph's snoring and those wide-eyed shepherds, loudly recounting angelic visitations. They probably woke the Baby several times that night. But, just before dawn, with all asleep except Mary and a mule, she gathered from the hope chest of the near past a tapestry of memories—the beautiful colors of Gabriel's clothes, the look on the face of Elizabeth when she turned and saw Mary, the clamor of packing for the dreaded tax appointment. No Vacancy signs, the nervous and frustrated father, the incarnate kicks, the looming grief, the tiny hands that would pierce her heart.

Mary wept and smiled, experiencing an orchestra of emotions in concert with the breeze that swept through the Bethlehem hills like a Spirit newly released. And Mary pondered. She rested in quiet peace and assurance. She loved God with all her heart. It was her most treasured gift.

What happens when you have a heart connection with God? You treasure it.

AWARE

Look inside your heart. Is your relationship with God based on tradition and rules, or is it a heart relationship with the one true God. Do you bow to Him out of simple duty, or do you treasure Him in your heart?

12 DAY Giving God Your Broken Heart

Others may fail you, but God will not.

"I love you. Do you love me?" Every person on the face of the planet has thought those words. As a third grader passes the universal note.

Do you love me? Circle one.   Yes   No   Maybe

We hear the golden oldies in the elevator: "How Do You Mend a Broken Heart?" "I Honestly Love You," "You've Lost that Lovin' Feelin'," "Your Cheatin' Heart," and so many others. You know, you'd think the world would have had enough of silly love songs. But why is it that we can't get enough of love. It is because we were created with a desire to love and be loved. Like peanut butter and jelly, we must also come to the realization that love and heartbreak go hand in hand.

The popular kid in school decides that you're the perfect victim of a humiliating nickname. The one you've been dying to date confesses that she'd rather study on a Saturday night than go with you anywhere. The one who promised to love you all the way to the altar gets cold feet and runs headlong into another relationship. The teacher you admire writes you off as a failure. The spouse of 20 years becomes disillusioned and wants out. The child you fed and clothed for 18 years thumbs his nose at your life, your home, and your Lord. You've prayed for your friend with cancer, certain that healing would come, but the answer from God comes in a funeral. You find yourself at the end of your life, alone in a forgotten assisted-living facility.

Heaviness. Pain. And a broken heart.

You might be at one of these crossroads today, and your heart feels like it will explode. The message for you is that God uses broken things, and He loves you in a way the world can't. The Bible says, "GOD's love, though, is ever and always, eternally present to all who fear him, making everything right for them and their children" (Ps. 103:17, *The Message*).

DARE
Accept God's love. Write your name in the blank. "For God so loved _____ that he gave his one and only Son, that whoever believes in him shall not perish but have eternal life" (John 3:16, NIV).

Passion Displayed

13 DAY

God calls us to fellowship in His suffering so self can find its way to the cross. Joy inexplicable resides in sacrifice of self (see Phil. 3:10).

The night before the crucifixion, the disciples didn't know the depth of His passion. Some were expecting a coronation. Some saw the eve of a battle or revolution. Only Jesus knew. He knew that the time had come for him to experience the greatest pain and deepest emotion any human had ever experienced or ever would. At this time of His greatest need, Jesus got up from the feast and wrapped a towel around His waist.

Imagine the reactions. "Master, please sit down! What are You doing? You're our leader. Put the towel back on the rack." Jesus poured water into a basin.

"Wait a minute, Jesus. We've seen You visit with lepers, Samaritans, and children. We've seen You spit in mud and deliver deranged demoniacs, but this is really uncalled for. You don't have to prove anything to us."

Jesus knelt at the feet of one whose feet were callused, scarred, and dusty from years of travel, and He began to wash them. A silence fell over the room. Only the sound of the water, the basin, the rag, and an occasional sob from those to whom He ministered.

He came to Peter, who adamantly refused, "No! You shall never wash my feet."

Jesus whispered, "Unless I wash you, you have no part with Me."

When Jesus finished washing the disciples' feet, he said: "Do you understand what I have done for you? You call Me 'Teacher' and 'Lord,' and rightly so, for that is what I am. Now that I, your Lord and Teacher, have washed your feet, you also should wash one another's feet. I have set you an example that you should do as I have done for you."

Son of God, Lord of the universe—approaching His greatest time of human need, His greatest moment of sacrifice—Jesus served with love, sorrow, passion. A passion for service. A passion for care. A passion for people. "Who, being in very nature God, did not consider equality with God something to be grasped, but made himself nothing, taking the very nature of a servant, being made in human likeness. And being found in appearance as a man, he humbled himself and became obedient to death—even death on a cross!" (Phil. 2:6-8, NIV).

Who will follow His leading? To serve out of passion, the passion portrayed that night—with a towel, a basin, water, and holy hands. Passion.

DECLARE
Spend some time today reading the Scriptures referred to above: John 13:1-17; Philippians 2:5-11; 3:10.

DAY 14 All Your Soul

God alone can satisfy your deepest longings.

SHARE

1. Have you ever collected anything? If so, what?

2. If you are not a collector, do you have a hobby, a major focus on a sport, another obsession?

- Tony is a major Tennessee Volunteers fan. Everything in his den is orange and white, and he has enough orange sweaters for the entire football team.
- Jennifer is a single adult who has just bought a home and remodeled the kitchen. Even though she seldom cooks, she bought top-of-the-line appliances and spent $50,000 on the kitchen renovation.
- Mike is addicted to video games. He spends all his extra money buying the latest games and all his extra time playing them.
- Teresa is an exercise and personal sports enthusiast. She has to have the latest equipment and the right clothes for each sport. She has mastered roller blades, a multispeed bike, racquetball, and spinning. She has a roomful of exercise equipment, and she's always looking for the next craze.
- Gus is an electronics gadget guru. His home office is an amazing collection of components, all wired together. Several computers are wired together for multiple Internet connections, so he can look for the next must-have software or hardware.
- Sue can't imagine a week without shopping. She has three pairs of shoes she's never taken out of the box and closets so full she can't remember what she owns.

DECLARE

1. Read Matthew 6:19-21:

"Don't collect for yourselves treasures on earth, where moth and rust destroy and where thieves break in and steal. But collect for yourselves treasures in heaven, where neither moth nor rust destroys, and where thieves don't break in and steal. For where your treasure is, there your heart will be also."

• What are you trying to gain, value, store up in life?

2. Read Luke 12:13-21:

Someone from the crowd said to Him, "Teacher, tell my brother to divide the inheritance with me."

"Friend," He said to him, "who appointed Me a judge or arbitrator over you?" And He told them, "Watch out and be on guard against all greed, because one's life is not in the abundance of his possessions."

Then He told them a parable: "A rich man's land was very productive. He thought to himself, 'What should I do, since I don't have anywhere to store my crops? I will do this,' he said. 'I'll tear down my barns and build bigger ones, and store all my grain and my goods there. Then I'll say to myself, "You have many goods stored up for many years. Take it easy; eat, drink, and enjoy yourself."'"

"But God said to him, 'You fool! This very night your life is demanded of you. And the things you have prepared—whose will they be?'

"That's how it is with the one who stores up treasure for himself and is not rich toward God."

• Circle the first-person pronouns (I, me, my, mine, myself).

Read Luke 12:19-20 in the *New American Standard Bible*:

"'And I will say to my soul, "Soul, you have many goods laid up for many years to come; take your ease, eat, drink and be merry."'

"But God said to him, 'You fool! This very night your soul is required of you; and now who will own what you have prepared?'" (NASB).

• Find and underline the word *soul*, used twice in this passage. Find the words used in place of *soul* in the HCSB.

• What do you think *soul* means?

• What does "This very night your soul is required of you" mean?

3. **Read Matthew 16:24-26:**

> Then Jesus said to his disciples, "If anyone would come after me, he must deny himself and take up his cross and follow me. For whoever wants to save his life will lose it, but whoever loses his life for me will find it. What good will it be for a man if he gains the whole world, yet forfeits his soul? Or what can a man give in exchange for his soul?" (NIV)

• What do you think "deny self" means?

• What do you need to deny yourself to follow Christ?

• What are some things in the world today that people appear to be exchanging for their souls?

4. **Read Psalm 103:3-13:**

> He forgives all your sin;
> He heals all your diseases.
> He redeems your life from the Pit;
> He crowns you with faithful love and compassion.
> He satisfies you with goodness;
> your youth is renewed like the eagle.
>
> The Lord executes acts of righteousness
> and justice for all the oppressed.
> He revealed His ways to Moses,
> His deeds to the people of Israel.
> The Lord is compassionate and gracious,
> slow to anger and full of faithful love.
> He will not always accuse us
> or be angry forever.
> He has not dealt with us as our sins deserve
> or repaid us according to our offenses.

For as high as the heavens are above the earth,
so great is His faithful love toward those who fear Him.
As far as the east is from the west,
so far has He removed our transgressions from us.
As a father has compassion on his children,
so the Lord has compassion on those who fear Him.

- What does God provide for you that you cannot provide for yourself?

DARE
Take inventory of the "stuff" in your life? Does it accurately reflect what you treasure?

CARE
Out of your abundance, how can you meet another's needs this week? at home? at work or among friends?

PRAYER
My soul, praise the LORD,
and all that is within me, praise His holy name.
My soul, praise the LORD,
and do not forget all His benefits (Ps. 103:1-2).

AWARE

Soul—Though it is often used in popular theology to refer only to the inner part of the person, the nonphysical aspect of each human being, it is used in other ways in Scripture, as well. In the Old Testament, the word sometimes indicates the whole person. It is also used to refer to the inner life, the psychological or spiritual states of the human person. In the New Testament, *soul* is often equated with the total person. It also indicates the emotions or passions. Jesus told the disciples that they should love God with all their souls, indicating something of the energy and passion that ought to go into loving Him. The New Testament also speaks of the soul as something that is distinguishable from the physical existence of a person.

Scripture clearly teaches that persons continue to exist consciously after physical death. Often *soul* is interchangeable with *spirit*. Spirit and soul are not different parts of the human but are the same.

There is a difference between body and soul, but the two are linked together by God so that humans are not complete when the two are separated.

Psyche—The New Testament word for *soul* is *psyche*, and the discipline called *psychology* was named after this Greek word. Psychology is literally the study of the soul.

Take up one's cross—Jesus established the primary figurative interpretation of the cross as a call to complete surrender to God. He used it five times as a symbol of true discipleship in terms of self-denial. Building upon the Roman practice of bearing the crossbeam to the place of execution, Jesus intended this in two directions: the death of self, involving the sacrifice of one's individuality for the purpose of following Jesus completely, and a willingness to imitate Jesus completely, even to the extent of martyrdom.

Scripture Text

Main Points

1.

2.

3.

Meaningful Illustrations

Personal Application

15 Not in Part
DAY but the Whole

In the sixties Bill Cosby performed a sketch about Noah.

The booming voice of God said, "Noah! Build an ark!"

Cosby, playing the part of Noah, said, "Right! Uh . . . what's an ark?"

Most people would be just as confused by the term *soul*. It's a word that carries a load of double meanings and clichés. Let's see. There's soul food, the king of soul, soul man, soul music, soul mates, and searching your soul. Playing a musical instrument with soul is the highest of compliments.

But what does the word mean when you read that God wants you to love Him with all your soul? It's hard to get our brains around the term because we don't think about soul the way people did in Bible times. So let's get on the same page. Think of it this way: you don't *have* a soul, you *are* a soul! *Soul* refers to the whole person. When Peter preached to the multitude on the day of Pentecost, three thousand souls were added to the church. That simply means three thousand people. *Soul* means all of you.

The New Testament (Greek) word for *soul* is *psyche*. That's where we get the word *psychology*. The word literally means "study of the soul." You can't separate your soul from what you think. You can't separate the brain from the body. The brain is simply hardware, and you are not just brain matter. Likewise, the soul is also physical. Many psychologists have tried to separate the two, but when you get right down to it, the process is impossible.

So what are the implications when God says He wants you to love Him with all your soul? He wants all of you. If you try to give Him a part and not the whole, you'll end up a wreck of a human being. Billions have tried. None have succeeded. They didn't follow God's plan: "Give your bodies to God. Let them be a living and holy sacrifice—the kind he will accept" (Rom. 12:1, NLT). Anything less than full surrender of the soul will lead you down a never-ending road of discontentment. Most people embrace an experiential life that accepts Jesus' existence but rebels at total surrender. Here's a vital question: What in your life are you holding back from the one true God who created you and knows you better than you know yourself?

AWARE

Sometime today take a minute or two to read Matthew 5:1-12. Ponder its meaning.

Spiritual Poverty 16 DAY

Blessed are the poor in spirit, because the kingdom of heaven is theirs (Matt. 5:3).

Jesus told this story to some men who were filled with great self-confidence and scorned everyone else:

"Two men went to the Temple to pray. One was a Pharisee, and the other was a dishonest tax collector. The proud Pharisee stood by himself and prayed this prayer: 'I thank you, God, that I am not a sinner like everyone else, especially like that tax collector over there! For I never cheat, I don't sin, I don't commit adultery, I fast twice a week, and I give you a tenth of my income.'

"But the tax collector stood at a distance and dared not even lift his eyes to heaven as he prayed. Instead, he beat his chest in sorrow, saying, 'O God, be merciful to me, for I am a sinner.' I tell you, this sinner, not the Pharisee, returned home justified before God. For the proud will be humbled, but the humble will be honored" (Luke 18:9-14, NLT).

What is the source of sin? It's a proud, self-ruling spirit. God didn't intend for us to be that way. To actualize true contentment, you must live a life ruled by God. When you get to the source, every human problem and sin comes because His rule was rejected.

Being poor in spirit means owning up to your sins. The Bible puts it this way: "You can't whitewash your sins and get by with it; you find mercy by admitting and leaving them" (Prov. 28:13, *The Message*).

Being poor in spirit means reaching the understanding that there is absolutely no way to live a fulfilling life outside of God. Paul the apostle said:

"Since we've compiled this long and sorry record as sinners (both us and them) and proved that we are utterly incapable of living the glorious lives God wills for us, God did it for us. Out of sheer generosity he put us in right standing with himself. A pure gift. He got us out of the mess we're in and restored us to where he always wanted us to be. And he did it by means of Jesus Christ" (Rom. 3:23-24, *The Message*).

PRAYER

Lord, Your Word says that You despise a proud-looking person. I turn away from my self-saving strategies, and I must confess that without You I'm a total loss. This is my spiritual desperation. I can do absolutely nothing without You. I am poor in spirit. Lord, help me. In the name of Jesus, the One who reached down to me. Amen.

17 Sorry or Sorrow
DAY

Blessed are those who mourn, because they will be comforted (Matt. 5:4).

Five-year-old twins are jumping on mom and dad's bed, having the time of their lives. Suddenly a loud crack ends the fun and games as they realize that something disastrous and fearful has happened.

"Mom and Dad are gonna be so mad."

They fear spankings, time-out, and, worst of all, no cartoons. Chills run down their spines as they hear dad's footsteps on the hardwood floor down the hall heading into the master bedroom. In unison they cry out, "He did it!"

Freddie says, "I'm sorry, I'm sorry! Pleeeease don't spank me!"

Teddy says, "I'm soooo sorry! I won't do it again. I promise! I'm sorry!"

Both are saying, "I'm sorry." But you know the truth. They're saying, "I'm sorry the bed broke, but I sure had fun jumping." This is not mourning. Mourning means recognizing your rebellion and sin. It means grief over your pride.

> For God can use sorrow in our lives to help us turn away from sin and seek salvation. We will never regret that kind of sorrow. But sorrow without repentance is the kind that results in death (2 Cor. 7:10, NLT).

Listen to the words of a man who committed unimaginable sin. Listen to the voice of true repentance. Listen to David, the king of Israel:

> Generous in love—God, give grace! Huge in mercy—wipe out my bad record. Scrub away my guilt, soak out my sins in your laundry. I know how bad I've been; my sins are staring me down. You're the One I've violated, and you've seen it all, seen the full extent of my evil. You have all the facts before you; whatever you decide about me is fair. I've been out of step with you for a long time, in the wrong since before I was born. What you're after is truth from the inside out. Enter me, then; conceive a new, true life (Ps. 51:1-6, *The Message*).

For every sin you confess, you will be forgiven. For every weakness you grieve over, you will receive strength and help. Those who mourn are blessed. They will be comforted. When you realize the extent to which you've been forgiven, your heart is changed, and you receive the strength and understanding to comfort others.

SHARE
The Bible says confess your fault one to another so that you may be healed. Is there a trusted friend with whom you can share a specific struggle with sin and ask for prayer. Take a moment today or this week to make that connection. It could change the status of your spiritual health.

The Right Kind of Strength and Hunger

DAY 18

Blessed are the meek: for they shall inherit the earth (Matt. 5:5, KJV).

What if someone described you as meek? It might not be a meant as a compliment. Words like *assertiveness* and *reckless power* are more favored. In Jesus' day *meek* meant "power under control." The picture painted in the word *meek* is that of a mighty thoroughbred at the gates, ready to run on the command of the one who holds the reigns.

Moses was described as meek (Num. 12:3, KJV). Aaron and Miriam questioned Moses' authority. They expressed an independent spirit. Moses could have defended himself. But he knew that God could take care of the situation. And God did, by striking them with a serious and loathsome illness! Moses allowed God to work, but he also prayed for Miriam's healing. The people rebelled again and again, but Moses never fought back. He knew God had a way to deal with them.

The world is crying out for men and women like Moses! Parents, teachers, politicians, and other leaders should trust God with a meek spirit when those under them rebel.

Blessed are those who hunger and thirst for righteousness, because they will be filled (Matt. 5:6).

Lord, why don't I long for You? My soul doesn't hunger and thirst for You. We worship You. You love us, and we love You, but hungering and thirsting is what I do for lasagna! And ice cream and Doritos®. My desire is for a nice house and clothes and a family.

Jesus said: "Don't hoard treasure down here where it gets eaten by moths and corroded by rust or—worse!—stolen by burglars. Stockpile treasure in heaven, where it's safe from moth and rust and burglars. It's obvious, isn't it? The place where your treasure is, is the place you will most want to be, and end up being" (Matt. 6:19-21, *The Message*).

Listen again to the lyrics of an ancient worship song: "As the deer pants for streams of water, so I long for you, O God. I thirst for God, the living God. When can I come and stand before him?" (Ps. 42:1-2, NLT).

If you hunger for God, you can rest assured that food will be on the way. Soul food!

PRAYER

Provider God, I confess that I need to stop being perpetually anxious about my life—what I should eat, drink, and wear. My life is greater than food, and my needs are greater than clothing. I know I can't live by bread alone. I hunger and thirst for the living Bread of life, in whose name I pray. Amen.

19 DAY — Mercy and Purity

Blessed are the merciful, because they will be shown mercy (Matt. 5:7).

The world's wisdom says if someone gets you, payback is coming. Our sinful nature thinks that way, and everyone struggles with the desire for revenge. God wants more from us! Jesus says, "Eye-for-an-eye religion? Not with Me." The best way to described mercy is to look at the ultimate example found in Bible. It's worth reading once more.

"But God showed his great love for us by sending Christ to die for us while we were still sinners" (Rom. 5:8, NIV).

"For God so greatly loved and dearly prized the world that He [even] gave up His only begotten (unique) Son, so that whoever believes in (trusts in, clings to, relies on) Him shall not perish (come to destruction, be lost) but have eternal (everlasting) life" (John 3:16, AMP).

God has His own list of the good, the bad, and the ugly. Wife abusers, child molesters, midnight cruisers, stock investors, honored marines, associate deans, chain smokers, flunkies, hash tokers, junkies, congressional page, victim of AIDS. Each soul can come clean!

Loving the Lord with all your soul means laying down the weapons of revenge and picking up the miracles of mercy, just as He did for us. Jesus said, if you show mercy, you will receive mercy. Let it be so!

Blessed are the pure in heart because they will see God (Matt. 5:8).

To love God with all your soul means to have a pure heart. A pure heart means an undivided heart. One that is sincere, not mixed. One that has a single focus, not two—or more. Jesus calls it a single eye. Luke calls it singleness of heart (Acts 2:46). James speaks of a double-minded man: "He is unstable in all his ways" (Jas. 1:8). A divided heart is disloyal. It tries to focus on both God and the world. You are to love the Lord with all your heart. It's the picture we have in athletics as the players wait for the jump ball, the runner waits for the gun, and the tennis player waits for the serve. We stand poised, focused, ready.

DARE

An old hymn says to turn your eyes upon Jesus. Are you skulking around this temporary rock called earth with a load of bitterness and a heart full of revenge, or are you a pure, peacemaking, God pursuer? The difference is night and day. The difference is life or death.

The Hard
Hopeful Truth

Blessed are the peacemakers, because they will be called sons of God (Matt. 5:9).

To be a peacemaker is to be like Jesus. Jesus is the Prince of peace (Isa. 9:6). When Jesus was born that first Christmas morning, the angels said He would bring peace to His people (Luke 2:14). Jesus comforted His disciples by saying, "Peace I leave with you. My peace I give to you" (John 14:27). The Bible also says, "For Christ himself has made peace between us Jews and you Gentiles by making us all one people. He has broken down the wall of hostility that used to separate us" (Eph. 2:14, NLT).

When we make peace, the world begins to see who our Father is—God Himself. To love the Lord with all your soul means that you are a peacemaker.

Blessed are those who are persecuted for righteousness, because the kingdom of heaven is theirs (Matt. 5:10).

Jesus ended these revolutionary words with a phrase that has turned the world upside-down. "Blessed are those who are persecuted because of righteousness, for theirs is the kingdom of heaven. Blessed are you when people insult you, persecute you and falsely say all kinds of evil against you because of me. Rejoice and be glad, because great is your reward in heaven, for in the same way they persecuted the prophets who were before you" (Matt. 6:10-12, NIV).

Facing persecution can come in different directions and at different levels. Eric Liddell, familiar from *Chariots of Fire*, loved to run. He felt God's pleasure when he ran. Torn between the call to missions and the call to honor God and country by racing, Liddell ultimately gave all he had for both areas of his life. His choice to obey God whatever the cost changed his life's course. It changed the race he would run and win. But the cost was great, ultimately leading him to China where he was arrested and died of starvation in a Chinese concentration camp.

Your persecution could come in the form of rejection or in being passed over for a promotion because you refuse to act unethically. You may face persecution in your own church or from bloodthirsty religious legalists like those Jesus faced and who are among us even today. Jesus' words are encouraging to people who face situations like these. The story isn't over. Rejoice. Jesus will have the final say.

DARE
Target your love toward an old enemy and see what God does!

21 DAY All Your Mind

The all-surpassing value in life is knowing Jesus.

SHARE

Share a piece of personal trivia that others in the group probably do not know (where you were born, a skill, a hobby).

Paul's resume could not be matched. His credentials? Flawless. Pedigree? He was born into the elite tribe of Benjamin. Saul, the first king of Israel, was from the tribe of Benjamin. Law abiding? He knew it. He lived it. He was a Pharisee (the best of the best). Religious? No one was more zealous. Righteous? No one could hold a stick to him. Add to that, he was multilingual, multicultural, and multitalented. But in Philippians he confesses that he'd trade his degrees, his trophies, his biographical history, and his entire profile as a grade-A, number-one, genius IQ for one thing: knowing Jesus. This, to Paul, was the ultimate—knowing Jesus now and forever.

Not only did Paul cash in his credentials for Jesus, but he also endured more than anyone you can imagine. He was frequently jailed, beaten, flogged, and shipwrecked. He spent a night treading water. He lived on the road. He was in danger from rivers, robbers, riptides, and rogues. Freezing, burning, and sleepless—Paul got the mother lode of bad breaks and hard times. His life from all earthly measurements was a tragedy. His friends deserted him. His fellow workers betrayed him. And three square meals were rarely on the radar. Why? One precious thing: "I want to know Christ!" (2 Cor. 11:22-33; 1 Cor. 2:2; Phil. 3:10).

DECLARE

1. **Read Philippians 3:4-6:**

   If anyone else thinks he has grounds for confidence in the flesh, I have more: circumcised the eighth day; of the nation of Israel, of the tribe of Benjamin, a Hebrew born of Hebrews; as to the law, a Pharisee; as to zeal, persecuting the church; as to the righteousness that is in the law, blameless.

- This is Paul's resume, his credentials. Make a list of items on your resume: accomplishments, education, impressive things about you you'd like others to know.

- Discuss ways people keep score today: power, academic degrees, fame, wealth, physical possessions, beauty. Add to the list.

2. Read Philippians 3:7:

But everything that was a gain to me, I have considered to be a loss because of Christ.

- Paul uses accounting terms, *gain* and *loss,* to place his life on a balance sheet. His assets, the gain side, included everything listed in verses 4-6. That was before he knew Christ. Knowing Jesus changed what Paul valued. His asset list then included only one item— knowing Christ. Has knowing Christ changed what you value?

3. Read Philippians 3:8:

More than that, I also consider everything to be a loss in view of the surpassing value of knowing Christ Jesus my Lord. Because of Him I have suffered the loss of all things and consider them filth, so that I may gain Christ.

- Paul's greatest gain is "knowing Christ Jesus," not knowing about Him. Is there a difference? If so, what is the difference

- When you created your resume, did you include being a Christian, knowing Christ, on it? Which of the items listed on your resume is more important than knowing Christ? Which do you value more? Which is your priority above knowing Christ?

- How does the way the world keeps score today differ from what Paul said has surpassing value?

4. Loving God with all your mind affects your attitude. **Read Philippians 2:5:**
    Let this mind be in you, which was also in Christ Jesus (KJV).

    Make your own attitude that of Christ Jesus (HCSB).

- Having the mind of Christ begins with accepting Him as Savior and beginning a relationship with Him, knowing Him (see the plan of salvation on page 88). Then you can begin to train your mind to become like His.

- What do you think it means to have the mind of Christ?

5. Read Philippians 2:3-4:
> Do nothing out of rivalry or conceit, but in humility consider others as more important than yourselves. Everyone should look out not only for his own interests, but also for the interests of others.

• How does Paul's instruction in these two verses compare with your description of the mind of Christ?

6. Read again the Greatest Commandment in Read Mark 12:29-31:
> Hear, O Israel! The Lord our God is one Lord. And you shall love the Lord your God with all your heart, with all your soul, with all your mind, and with all your strength. . . .You shall love your neighbor as yourself.

• Which part of the Greatest Commandment is reflected in Philippians 2?

7. A Christian's thought life should differ from that of a person who is not a Christian.
Read Proverbs 23:7:
> As he thinks within himself, so he is.

• How do your thoughts shape who you are? Do your thoughts reflect the mind of Christ?

• What are some things you can do (or not do) to train your mind to be like His?

8. Read Philippians 4:8 to discover ideas for training your mind to be like His:
> Finally brothers, whatever is true, whatever is honorable, whatever is just, whatever is pure, whatever is lovely, whatever is commendable—if there is any moral excellence and if there is any praise—dwell on these things.

Read Romans 12:2:
> Do not be conformed to this age, but be transformed by the renewing of your mind, so that you may discern what is the good, pleasing, and perfect will of God.

• In what ways do Christians today conform to the culture in which they live?

• Christians must depend on God to transform their minds so that they may discern what pleases Him. Write one attitude or thought you would like God to change in you.

DARE

1. What in your life should be trivial that you have made significant?

2. What in your life should be significant that you have made trivial?

CARE

Reread Philippians 2:3-4:
Do nothing out of rivalry or conceit, but in humility consider others as more important than yourselves. Everyone should look out not only for his own interests, but also for the interests of others.

• How can you put the needs of others above your own this week? in your family? among friends and coworkers? at church?

PRAYER

And I pray this: that your love will keep on growing in knowledge and every kind of discernment, so that you can determine what really matters and can be pure and blameless in the day of Christ (Phil. 1:9-10).

AWARE

Know, knowledge—The Greek concept of knowing was primarily intellectual. It was information based, intellectual understanding. This reflects the way contemporary culture uses these terms.

The Hebrew concept of knowing was experiential and relational. The Hebrew concept was what Paul had in mind when he wrote about knowing Jesus in Philippians 3. The Hebrew concept closely reflects the totality of loving God as described in the Greatest Commandment.

Mind—The center of intellectual activity, an English term translating several different Hebrew and Greek terms. The New Testament has a large number of terms which are used to describe mankind's "faculty of cognition." As in the Old Testament, the term *heart (kardia)* is sometimes used to represent the concept *mind* (see Matt. 13:15).

Mind is sometimes associated with the human soul (see Phil. 1:27; Heb. 12:3; Acts 14:2, for example). These passages illustrate the fact that the mind is considered to be the center of the person. However, in Scripture the heart is more often considered to be the center of the human personality. In the Old Testament especially, this is true because of the lack of an exact equivalent for *mind*. The word *heart* fills this void, and the New Testament follows the practice of the Old Testament closely. Why then can the mind as well as the heart be spoken of as the center of a person? Because in Hebrew thought a person is looked at as a single entity with no attempt to compartmentalize the person into separate parts which act more or less independently of one another. Therefore, the heart, mind, and soul, while in some ways different, are seen as one.

The mind is often portrayed, especially in the New Testament, as the center of one's ethical nature. The mind can be evil (Rom. 1:28; Col. 2:18; Eph. 4:17; 1 Tim. 6:5; 2 Tim. 3:8; Titus 1:15). Yet we are commanded to love God with all our minds. This is possible because the mind can be revived and empowered by the Holy Spirit (Rom. 12:2) and because God's laws under the new covenant are put into our minds (Heb. 8:10; 10:16).

Mind of Christ—T. W. Hunt and Claude V. King list six characteristics of the Christlike mind:
1. *Alive*—"For the mind-set of the flesh is death, but the mind-set of the Spirit is life and peace" (Rom. 8:6).
2. *Single-minded*—"But I fear that . . . your minds may be corrupted from a complete and pure devotion to Christ" (2 Cor. 11:3).
3. *Lowly*—"Do nothing out of rivalry or conceit, but in humility consider others as more important than yourselves" (Phil. 2:3).
4. *Pure*—"To the pure, everything is pure, but to those who are defiled and unbelieving nothing is pure; in fact, both their mind and conscience are defiled" (Titus 1:15).
5. *Responsive*—"Then He opened their minds to understand the Scriptures" (Luke 24:45).
6. *Peaceful*—"For the mind-set of the flesh is death, but the mind-set of the Spirit is life and peace" (Rom. 8:6).

Scripture Text

Main Points
1.

2.

3.

Meaningful Illustrations

Personal Application

22 DAY The Christlike Mind Is Alive and at Peace

"The mind of sinful man is death, but the mind controlled by the Spirit is life and peace" (Rom. 8:6, NIV). Without Christ we are dead.

> It wasn't so long ago that you were mired in that old stagnant life of sin. You let the world, which doesn't know the first thing about living, tell you how to live (Eph. 2:1-2, *The Message*).

> That is why whoever accepts and trusts the Son gets in on everything, life complete and forever! And that is also why the person who avoids and distrusts the Son is in the dark and doesn't see life. All he experiences of God is darkness, and an angry darkness at that (John 3:36, *The Message*).

Jesus lined out the kind of life you can have if you really want to live life at its best. "The thief comes only in order to steal and kill and destroy. I came that they may have and enjoy life, and have it in abundance (to the full, till it overflows)" (John 10:10, AMP).

Surely that's the kind of life you want. And when you set your mind on the spirit and the mind of Christ, that's the kind of life you can get.

The mind of Christ is a mind of peace. Peace is a fruit of the spirit, not an attainment. Your work is setting your mind (Rom. 8:5-6). God's work is providing peace. Jesus had peace. Remember what He said? "Come to me, all of you who are weary and carry heavy burdens, and I will give you rest" (Matt. 11:28, NLT).

Jean Sophie Pigott, a 19th-century poet, described this life of peace brilliantly:

Jesus, I am resting, resting,
In the joy of what You are.
I am finding out the greatness
Of Your loving heart.
You have bid me gaze upon You,
And Your beauty fills my soul,
For by Your transforming power,
You have made me whole.

Simply trusting You, Lord Jesus,
I behold You as You are.
And Your love, so pure, so changeless,
Satisfies my heart;
Satisfies its deepest longings,
Meets, supplies its every need,
Circles me around with blessings:
Yours is love indeed!

DARE

What part of your life brings moments where you feel conflicted? Ask God to lift those things from your shoulders. He is speaking through eternity directly to you. He's saying, "Release those burdens and struggles. Lay them at My feet."

The Monster of Regret

Is it possible to have a new mind despite having a jaded past?

Perhaps the most difficult thing for Christians to do is to accept their sinful acts and wrong choices of the past. What events or things in your past have made you hesitant even to try to be open to God? Maybe there are events in your past that you could not control. Perhaps you were abused as a child. Or maybe your parents divorced during your teenage years, and the hurt that you feel seems overwhelming and impossible to escape. Even in the most ideal circumstances, people carry burdens from unanticipated grief, sorrow, and crises.

One more thing. Are there issues of unforgiveness in your life that have driven a wedge between you and God?

If you truly ponder these areas, God may bring you into a new understanding of your spiritual condition. The good news is that God has the ability to bring you into a new mind that is free from the monster of regret. In his book *In the Grip of Grace,* Max Lucado has these words for the one who struggles with the mind of the past. "Where the grace of God is missed, bitterness is born. But where the grace of God is embraced, forgiveness flourishes."

What's God's promise? "If we confess our sins, he is faithful and just and will forgive us our sins and purify us from all unrighteousness" (1 John 1:9, NIV). "'Come now, let us reason together,' says the LORD. 'Though your sins are like scarlet, they shall be as white as snow; though they are red as crimson, they shall be like wool'" (Isa. 1:18, NIV). "Bear with each other and forgive whatever grievances you may have against one another. Forgive as the Lord forgave you" (Col. 3:13, NIV). "As far as the east is from the west, so far has he removed our transgressions from us" (Ps. 103:12, NIV).

Allow God's grace to amaze your mind.

PRAYER

Lord, I praise You for being a God who forgives. I desperately need to know and understand the depth of Your forgiveness. I confess these areas of my life where I have failed to seek Your forgiveness and to forgive others. Lord Jesus, more than anything I want to have a pure and holy life. I want to have an intimate relationship with You. Cleanse me and make me the holy servant You desire. I understand that I cannot be holy on my own. I am reaching out to You in the best way I know how. I want You to take me, break me, and renew my mind. In Jesus' name. Amen.

24 DAY A Beautiful Mind

History proves that there is a great difference between intelligence and wisdom.

You can have enormous riches and still fall into fits of anxiety and fear.

You can be a world leader and still be sexually addicted.

You can be a CEO, yet end your life in total regret.

You can be a poet bound for textbooks and still live a life void of happiness.

A beautiful mind is a lowly mind. It has little to do with accounts, achievements, and awards. The Bible says:

> Do nothing from factional motives [through contentiousness, strife, selfishness, or for unworthy ends] or prompted by conceit and empty arrogance. Instead, in the true spirit of humility (lowliness of mind) let each regard the others as better than and superior to himself [thinking more highly of one another than you do of yourselves] (Phil. 2:3, AMP).

The opposite of lowliness is arrogance. Lowliness is a trait to cultivate. What's the key to developing lowliness of mind? The secret is a focus on God. Start there. If you want to see God move dynamically in the intimate details of your life as well as in the gigantic contentions of the world, you must become lowly.

Individual things?

> For though the Lord is high, yet has He respect to the lowly [bringing them into fellowship with Him]; but the proud and haughty He knows and recognizes [only] at a distance (Ps. 138:6, AMP).

Big things?

> If My people, who are called by My name, shall humble themselves, pray, seek, crave, and require of necessity My face and turn from their wicked ways, then will I hear from heaven, forgive their sin, and heal their land (2 Chron. 7:14, AMP).

PRAYER

Lord, Let this mind be in me, which was also in Jesus.

Do Whatever He Tells You to Do!

The mind that is inhabited by Christ listens and responds to Him.

Have you ever had a dog that loved you completely? Cats, I'm convinced, aren't capable of that kind of devotion, but sometimes you'll find that kind of dog. Ready to please and watching your every move, this dog totally understands the word *master*. What is easy for some dogs is difficult for most Christians. Being responsive to Christ takes faith and a new mind.

Perhaps the greatest advice from a mother is tucked away in the Gospel of John, chapter 2. It came from the mouth of the mother of our Lord. It wasn't a life or death situation. It was a party. At first glance the words had little to do with eternal destinies or climactic discoveries—just a simple statement in the midst of uncertain, perplexing, awkward circumstances. When poorly planned catering led to an embarrassing lack of liquid refreshment, Mary saw the empty pitchers and said to the servants, "Do whatever He tells you to do." She knew exactly who her Son was. She pointed to Jesus, and with determination and authority in her voice, she said, "Do whatever He tells you to do!"

Imagine the scene. "Fill the pots with water," He told them. They protested.

Mary looked on, perhaps assertively with arms crossed. She said it again. "Do whatever He tells you to do." They filled the pots.

Then Jesus said, "Now draw some out and take it to the master of the banquet."

"You're joking, right?" a cynical servant asked with a coy smile.

"Do whatever He tells you to do," Mary repeated.

At that moment Jesus transformed the ordinary into the extraordinary. If you listen closely, perhaps you can hear the words of that proud and courageous mother. Her words still apply. *Do whatever He tells you to do.* As you minister to the homeless, *do whatever He tells you to do.* As you follow Him to a foreign land, *do whatever He tells you to do.* As you budget your time and resources, *do whatever He tells you to do.* As you proclaim the good news wherever you go, *do whatever He tells you to do!*

This mother's advice through years of weddings, funerals, challenges, and crises, in the big things, in the little things, in the plans for today and the dreams of tomorrow—is really some very good advice. Do whatever He tells you to do!

AWARE

It may seem strange. It might go against your natural instincts. But respond. Do whatever He tells you to do. What *is* He telling you to do?

26 Your Mind:
DAY A Place for God

"You may not be what you think you are, but you are what you think." This statement challenges us to live a life that is refreshingly different. Its premise is based on Bible truth:

> Whatever is true, whatever is noble, whatever is right, whatever is pure, whatever is lovely, whatever is admirable—if anything is excellent or praiseworthy—think about such things (Phil. 4:8, NIV).

When we focus on God things, earth things become insignificant. Look at the earth things around you—your car, your home, the grass that you can't seem to get free of weeds, your gadgets, your hair, your jewelry, your food. Eventually, it's all going to go away. Every car will stop running. Every crust of food will be eaten or discarded. Every toy will break. Even your earthly problems and anxieties will eventually go away, usually to be replaced by other problems and irritants. Eternity will make a victim of everything that's not in Christ.

Paul's advice to us is this:

> Don't shuffle along, eyes to the ground, absorbed with the things right in front of you. Look up, and be alert to what is going on around Christ—that's where the action is. See things from his perspective (Col. 3:2, *The Message*).

This is indeed the mind of Christ. It's what really counts. Beth Moore says, "The question is not, 'Is Jesus the One and Only?' Our vote cannot elect Him to a position He already occupies. The question is this: Has Jesus become *your* One and Only?"

Is your mind focused on what this life is all about? Have the things of the earth grown strangely dim? I haven't met a person who was so heavenly minded that he was no earthly good. I couldn't begin to count the number of people who were so earthly minded they were no heavenly good. In fact, I've been at that place a time or two myself. To be honest, a lot more than I'd like to admit.

God is asking you to renew your mind and turn heavenward. Right now.

> When we look to the sky
> And He appears with a shout
> No one will deny
> What this life's all about.

DARE

Give one earthly treasure to someone as a symbol that God is moving your eyes from earthly stuff to eternal glory.

The Single-Minded Life

One of our spiritual problems is becoming spiritually distracted or being "led astray." "But I fear that somehow you will be led away from your pure and simple devotion to Christ, just as Eve was deceived by the serpent" (2 Cor. 11:3, NLT). Our minds dart in hundreds of directions. We're bombarded by distractions. Sensory overload numbs our minds. Single-mindedness is a choice. So is the opposite: "All of us have strayed away like sheep. We have left God's paths to follow our own" (Isa. 53:6, NLT).

The single-minded Christian pays attention to Christ. His commands. His Person. His ways. Isaiah noted, "You will keep in perfect peace all who trust in you, whose thoughts are fixed on you" (Isa. 26:3, NLT). It is a preoccupation with sincere, pure devotion to Christ. King David prayed: "I'm asking GOD for one thing, only one thing: To live with him in his house my whole life long. I'll contemplate his beauty; I'll study at his feet" (Ps. 27:4, *The Message*).

When multitasking seems to be the on-demand solution for everything, why is single-minded living so important? Because "[God] is the one who made heaven and earth, the sea, and everything in them. He is the one who keeps every promise forever" (Ps. 146:6, NLT). Now that is consistency!

DARE

You know the mantra. Time is money. If your week could be compared to money and every week of your life were equal to $500, how much of that $500 would be spend in spiritual renewal? What amount would be spent on TV and radio? What percentage would be spent in exhausting, nonproductive activities? Pick a couple of these exercises that express your commitment to the single-minded life:

- Remain silent before the Lord for 15 minutes.
- Say, "Good morning, Lord," when you wake up.
- Put the television in the attic for a month.
- Pledge not to buy an article of clothing for yourself for six months.
- Pick an amount of time to fast this week.

28 DAY All Your Strength

In God's strength you can do anything.

Early on the morning of May 27, 2001, missionaries Martin and Gracia Burnham were seized at gunpoint while celebrating their wedding anniversary at an island resort in the Philippines. For more than a year, they were held captive in the jungle by a terrorist group thought to have ties to Osama bin Laden. The Burnhams faced exhaustion and starvation, and Martin was often chained to a tree at night. Through their ordeal they relied on each other and on God. Martin was killed and Gracia was injured by indiscriminate fire from government troops, attempting to rescue them. Gracia's testimony today continues to be that God saw her through her captivity and continues to sustain her today.

Lisa Beamer, homemaker, mother, and the widow of Todd Beamer, who died to stop the 9-11 terrorist aboard his American Airlines flight, has become a national symbol of strength, a symbol of unshaken faith. Lisa said: "God doesn't want bad things to happen to us, but He doesn't always stop them either. He has plans that are bigger than anything we can determine for ourselves. And so, in the midst of whatever's happening to us, He continues to love us and take care of us. He has a plan for us, and certainly He is preparing an eternity for us."

David Ring's life tells his story. "When I was born, the oxygen couldn't get to my brain, so I have cerebral palsy. That's why I walk with a limp and talk like I do—because of cerebral palsy at birth." Remarkably, despite a devastating disability and the scorn of childhood friends, David became a teacher and evangelist, traveling to hundreds of churches each year.

You can add your own stories of childless mothers, martyred believers, and victims of abuse and violence who could easily shout, "This is not what I signed up for! God, how could you watch this happen and do nothing." Still, like Gracia Burnham, Lisa Beamer, and David Ring, they courageously, consistently have the strength to overcome and carry out the mission of their lives.

How?

SHARE

1. Tell about a time you have felt strong.

2. Tell about a time you have felt weak.

3. What pictures come to mind when you think of powerful, successful people? How do these images sometimes conflict with the teachings of Jesus?

DECLARE

1. Read about overcoming weaknesses in 2 Corinthians 12:7-10:

Therefore, so that I would not exalt myself, a thorn in the flesh was given to me, a messenger of Satan to torment me so I would not exalt myself. Concerning this, I pleaded with the Lord three times to take it away from me. But He said to me, "My grace is sufficient for you, for power is perfected in weakness." Therefore, I will most gladly boast all the more about my weaknesses, so that Christ's power may reside in me. So because of Christ, I am pleased in weaknesses, in insults, in catastrophes, in persecutions, and in pressures. For when I am weak, then I am strong.

• Paul had a weakness, a _____ in the flesh.

• Verse 10 mentions a number of areas where God's strength is needed. Beside each area listed below, name a specific need for God's strength that fits that category today.

Weaknesses _____

Insults _____

Catastrophes _____

Persecutions _____

Pressures _____

• Discuss these types of circumstances. Circle one you are facing today.

• In this case God did not remove Paul's thorn in the flesh, but He did give him the grace to sustain him. What God did for Paul He will do for you. Discuss how this is true for the examples at the beginning of the session.

2. Paul faced many adversities, but he no longer measured success by possessions or circumstances. **Read about it in Philippians 4:10-13:**

I rejoiced in the Lord greatly that now at last you have renewed your care for me. You were, in fact, concerned about me, but lacked the opportunity to show it. I don't say this out of need, for I have learned to be content in whatever circumstances I am. I know both how to have a little, and I know how to have a lot. In any and all circumstances I have learned the secret of being content—whether well-fed or hungry, whether in abundance or in need. I am able to do all things through Him who strengthens me.

- Among the things the Apostle Paul attempted are these: teacher, missionary, evangelist, church planter, letter writer, discipler, mentor. When circumstances, like being in prison, kept him from public evangelism, he wrote letters of encouragement and instruction to the churches he had established. Wherever he was, he found a way to serve God. He could have made excuses like these:
  - ❏ I'm too young and inexperienced.
  - ❏ I have a sinful past.
  - ❏ I'm too busy.
  - ❏ I've never done this before.
  - ❏ I've had my turn; let someone else do it.
  - ❏ I'm tired.
  - ❏ I tried this once before, and all I got was criticism.
  - ❏ I'm too old.

  Discuss these and other reasons people give for not serving God. If one of these, applies to you, place a checkmark by it. If another reason is holding you back from serving, write it here.

Remember that you can do all things through Christ who gives you strength.

3. God's strength is a renewable resource. **Read about God's renewing strength in Isaiah 40:31:**

   But those who hope in the LORD will renew their strength. They will soar on wings like eagles; they will run and not grow weary, they will walk and not be faint (NIV).

- You may have been attempting great things for God for a long time, and you may feel that your energy is gone. Perhaps you have been working in your own strength rather than God's. Recall a time your energy was depleted and you were able to continue only in God's strength.

When you love the Lord with all your strength, you attempt what He asks you to do out of love and obedience to Him. He in turn provides the strength to sustain you.

4. **Read Ephesians 6:10:**

   Finally, be strengthened by the Lord and by His vast strength.

DARE

William Carey (1761–1834), a Baptist missionary, frequently preached: "Expect great things from God. Attempt great things for God."

What is God asking you to attempt for Him? Write it here:

If you attempt what God wants you to do, what kinds of help or strength would you need from God?

CARE

Read Acts 14:21-22:

> After they had evangelized that town and made many disciples, they returned to Lystra, to Iconium, and to Antioch, strengthening the hearts of the disciples by encouraging them to continue in the faith, and by telling them, "It is necessary to pass through many troubles on our way into the kingdom of God."

One way to express your love to God with all your strength is to encourage your brothers and sisters in Christ. What can you do this week to encourage a fellow disciple who is passing through many troubles to continue in the faith?

PRAYER

O LORD, be gracious to us; we long for you. Be our strength every morning, our salvation in time of distress (Isa. 33:2, NIV).

AWARE

Thorn in the flesh—The Greek word *skolops* occurred in classical Greek as a stake or sharp wooden shaft used to impale. In Hellenistic Greek the variations *thorn* and *splinter* are found.

Paul's revelation was balanced by a "thorn in the flesh." During this era physical ailments were a constant problem. As a result, most church fathers perceived Paul's affliction as either a painful, chronic physical problem or ongoing persecution.

Four modern theories concern Paul's thorn in the flesh. The most common theory is some sort of recurring physical illness, possibly malaria. Some hold that Paul suffered from an eye disease. A third common theory was sorrow and pain because of Jewish unbelief. A fourth theory is that of a "messenger of Satan," rather than a physical ailment, given as a redemptive judgment of God on Paul for the purpose of keeping Paul humble.

Sermon Notes / **All Your Strength**

Scripture Text

Main Points

1.

2.

3.

Meaningful Illustrations

Personal Application

"Haven't I commanded you? Strength! Courage! Don't be timid; don't get discouraged. GOD, your God, is with you every step you take" (Josh. 1:9, *The Message*).

The simple message today could be summed up in two words: We win! When you were adopted by Father God, you claimed a share of the winner's prize. Listen to these victory shouts:

"Overwhelming victory is ours through Christ, who loved us" (Rom. 8:37, NLT).

Notice: Christ allowed us to share in the win!

"But thanks be to God, who made us his captives and leads us along in Christ's triumphal procession. Now wherever we go he uses us to tell others about the Lord and to spread the Good News like a sweet perfume" (2 Cor. 2:14, NLT).

Notice: You are His success story!

"O Israel, hope in the LORD; for with the LORD there is unfailing love and an overflowing supply of salvation" (Ps. 130:7, NLT).

Notice: You can count on there being plenty of salvation to go around. God's grace is not in short supply.

In *Life in the Spirit*, Robertson McQuilken put it like this, "We're not condemned as human beings to live a life of spiritual failure. We must resist those who push us back into the fog of defeat. The Bible is clear that God doesn't expect absolute perfection in this life, though He does promise that in heaven we will be like Him, for we shall see Him as He is (1 John 3:2)."

In the meantime what can we expect?

McQuilken went on to say that we can expect, with God's strength, to win over temptations to choose wrong and to grow steadily toward greater likeness to Jesus in our attitudes and actions.

DARE

What sin or temptation has been getting the upper hand in your life? Here's your two-part challenge:

1. Pray right now. Ask God to give you His power and His Spirit to be victorious.
2. Tell a friend. Be accountable to someone you trust who will pray for you and check up on you.

Why God Shouldn't Use You

You may say, "There are many reasons God shouldn't use me." You're right! But don't worry. You're in good company. Moses stuttered. David's armor didn't fit. John Mark was rejected by Paul. Timothy had ulcers. Hosea's wife was a prostitute. Amos's only training was in the school of fig tree pruning. Jacob was a liar. David had an affair. Solomon was too rich. Abraham was too old. David was too young. Peter was afraid of death. Lazarus was dead. Naomi was a widow. Jonah ran from God. Miriam was a gossip. Gideon and Thomas both doubted. Jeremiah was depressed. Elijah was burned out. John the Baptist was a loudmouth. Martha was a worrywart. Mary was lazy. Samson had long hair. Noah got drunk. Did I mention that Moses had a short fuse? So did Peter and Paul; well, lots of folks did.

But God doesn't require a job interview. He doesn't hire and fire like most bosses because He's more our dad than our boss. He doesn't look at financial gain or loss. He's not prejudiced or partial. Not judging, grudging, sassy, or brassy, not deaf to our cry, not blind to our need. As much as we try to earn them, God's gifts are free. We could do wonderful things for wonderful people and still not be wonderful. Satan says, "You're not worthy." Jesus says, "So what? I am." Satan looks back and sees our mistakes. God looks back and sees the cross. He doesn't calculate what you did in '98. It's not even on the record. Sure, there are lots of reasons God can't use you. But if you are in love with Him, if you hunger for Him more than your next breath, He'll use you. It's a given. So today, step out of your limitations.

It's all about a God who works through you. He says:

> I will go before you and will level the mountains; I will break down gates of bronze and cut through bars of iron. I will give you the treasures of darkness, riches stored in secret places, so that you may know that I am the LORD, the God of Israel, who summons you by name (Isa. 45:2-3, NIV).

DARE

Make a list of all the excuses you have for not loving God with all your strength and find a symbolic way to turn those excuses over to Him. They are as dangerous as anything in keeping you from accomplishing the Great Commandment.

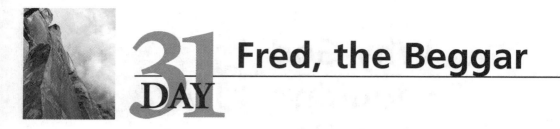

God has a better plan and more resources.

Fred collected cans and recyclable bottles in an old grocery cart that needed a serious wheel alignment. His diet consisted mainly of canned dog food and, on special occasions, Spam. It wasn't a victorious life by any stretch of the imagination. Until one day an attorney visited his cardboard shack. He had good news.

"Fred! Your troubles are over! An uncle you never met died last week. He left $2 million to your father, who died last year, which means that the money is yours."

Wall Street investors rushed to his side. Women suddenly somehow found Fred attractive. Reporters asked, "You won $2 million! What are you gonna do?"

"I've got a plan. I'm going to buy new cardboard for this old place. I'm going to eat brand-name dog food and Spam! It's been so long since I had fried Spam for breakfast!"

He was a millionaire who didn't understand. He couldn't look beyond his slum life into a new life. In the following days he was swindled out of every dollar he inherited.

Many believers have lived their entire lives with Fred's worldview. Perhaps you are trying to live life by your own strategy when Jesus came to give you overflowing, abundant life. The secret is to love God, using your strength the way Jesus did. Think of it. Three years and Jesus, through the power of the Father and the fellowship of the Spirit, turned the world upside down. We set our calendars by His birth.

Fred is ficticious. Jim Elliott is real. Jim accepted the challenge to be like Christ, and his life had eternal significance. A missionary to the South America, where he was brutally martyred at the age of 28, Jim once said, "Wherever you are, be all there. Live to the hilt every situation you believe to be the will of God."

Are you willing to live your life with the same fire, enthusiasm, and passion as Jim? God may not call you to dodge the arrows of a godless tribe in the jungles of South America, but are you willing to be a living sacrifice? to express your spiritual gifts in high gear? Are you ready to live this life to the hilt for the Jesus' sake?

Listen to a prophet of old repeat words from God: "Don't let the wise brag of their wisdom. Don't let heroes brag of their exploits. Don't let the rich brag of their riches. If you brag, brag of this and this only: That you understand and know me" (Jer. 9:23-24, *The Message*).

DARE
Write a prayer to God, committing to live life to the hilt as you seize the gifts He has given you.

Five Questions

As Christians, we carry around in our bodies the death of Jesus, so that the life of Jesus may also be revealed in us (2 Cor. 4:10). In other words we are containers of Christ Himself. On the other end of the spectrum, Satan realizes that if he can shorten our lives or weaken our energy to love God, he can ultimately strike a mortal blow to the very reason for our existence.

Brennan Manning says, "The greatest single cause of atheism in the world today is Christians who acknowledge Jesus with their lips, then walk out the door and deny Him by their lifestyle. That is what an unbelieving world simply finds unbelievable."

Take a strength test. (No weights or personal trainer needed!) Just five questions:

1. Am I leading a restless life? People are working more these days than ever before. The inability to unplug from the stresses of activity and the inability to get the proper amount of sleep and refreshment can compromise your ability to love the Lord with all your strength.

Which of these statements are true in your life?
- I'm constantly on the move from one promise to the next.
- I'm up late and rolling out of bed early almost every day.
- I have more invitations than I have time.
- I feel that God is most pleased when I am busy.

I recently saw a church sign that displayed the following statement. "Jesus is coming. Look busy!" No kidding. It is as true as it is sad and absurd.

2. Do I lead a passive life? Are you a mouse potato, sitting in front of the computer eight hours a day? Do you honor your body's physical needs? Loving God with all your strength means investing time in a healthy temple.

3. Are you eating intentionally? What are your eating habits? Are you an overeater, a carboholic, a fast-food junkie?

4. Are you addicted to drugs, chemicals, or obsessive habits?

5. Do you have sexual integrity? Is pornography, adultery, premarital sex, an emotional affair, or sexual escapism playing a role in your life?

PRAYER

Lord, I acknowledge that You are the strength of my life. My body is a temple of the Holy Spirit. I commit to love You with all of my strength and to walk in truth and integrity. I commit my energies to You. I will come to You, and You will give me rest. I can do all things through Your Son, Christ, who gives me strength.

33 DAY — God's Applause

Madonna and Mother Teresa—two women with totally different approaches to life.

Madonna has made millions pursuing self-satisfaction. The world deems her a success because of the millions she has amassed—and, perhaps, because of the millions of people she has made gasp in response to her provocative behavior.

Mother Teresa rarely had two coins to rub together during her lifetime, and if she did, she gave them to the poor. But with a heart like His, she dedicated herself to pouring out God's love to everyone she met. Doing so wasn't her work; it was her life.

What about you? You can slouch in front of the latest reality show. You can rush to the latest game, show, or book; or you can choose to get in the game. Your primary responsibility is to ensure that *your* life will count for something. You can choose to live a life that makes a difference.

Paul described such a life:

> You're going to find that there will be times when people will have no stomach for solid teaching, but will fill up on spiritual junk food—catchy opinions that tickle their fancy. They'll turn their backs on truth and chase mirages (2 Tim. 4:3-4, *The Message*).

But not so with Paul. What Christian doesn't admire Paul's confession to Timothy: "This is the only race worth running. I've run hard right to the finish, believed all the way. All that's left now is the shouting—God's applause!" (2 Tim. 4:7-8, *The Message*). What a finish!

PRAYER

Lord, teach me what it means to finish strong. I don't want to live my life vicariously, moving from one distraction to another. I don't want to toil away in the muck of the mundane. Lord, I choose to live the extraordinary life of a God-empowered chaser of holy dreams and passionate missions.

Lord, crush my sense of self-significance and replace it with an eternal conversation with your Son. And may I always choose God's applause over the fool's gold of earthbound acclaim.

Who Gets the Glory

The credit for eternal blessings belongs to God.

Anyone who has spent a significant amount of time playing with three-year-olds has probably heard, "I'll do it myself." Diction and pronunciation may vary. They might even say it through a nonverbal stance or a frustrated expression. But most children want to do it themselves. I'm convinced they'd want to drive the car if we'd let them. Theirs is a world of innate experimentation and fantasy.

As a believer, I catch myself falling into that same trap spiritually. "I'll do it myself, Lord," I say as I try to win someone's heart through theological debate. "I'll do it myself," I whisper to the Lord through my actions at church. "I'll do it myself, Lord," as I discipline my kids, balance the family budget, and try (fruitlessly) to control my spouse's attitude.

When we try to take the credit for our victories, we make the Christian walk absurd. Our life on earth is simply rehearsal for heaven. We don't know all that awaits us, but we do know who will get the glory. There will be a time in the near future when we'll proclaim with the angels, "The Lamb (Jesus) is worthy—the Lamb who was killed. He is worthy to receive power and riches and wisdom and strength and honor and glory and blessing" (Rev. 5:12, NLT).

Paul shared his secret with the Galatians:

> My ego is no longer central. It is no longer important that I appear righteous before you or have your good opinion, and I am no longer driven to impress God. Christ lives in me. The life you see me living is not "mine," but it is lived by faith in the Son of God, who loved me and gave himself for me (Gal. 2:20, *The Message*).

The greatest traps for Christians are not found in the dark alleys of trouble but rather when we feel most confident. God put a warning label on prosperity and self-confidence before the promised land was ever seen:

> For when you have become full and prosperous and have built fine homes to live in, and when your flocks and herds have become very large and your silver and gold have multiplied along with everything else, that is the time to be careful. Do not become proud at that time and forget the LORD your God, who rescued you from slavery in the land of Egypt (Deut. 8:12-14, NLT).

CARE

Give glory to God during your moments of triumph by empathizing and ministering to the downtrodden.

35 DAY Love Your Neighbor

You should love others as much as you love yourself.

SHARE

Who are your neighbors?

Have you ever had an emergency and needed help from strangers? What happened?

DECLARE

Read the story of the good Samaritan in Luke 10:25-37:

> Just then an expert in the law stood up to test Him, saying, "Teacher, what must I do to inherit eternal life?"
>
> "What is written in the law?" He asked him. "How do you read it?"

He answered:

> You shall love the Lord your God with all your heart, with all your soul, with all your strength, and with all your mind; and your neighbor as yourself.

> "You've answered correctly," He told him. "Do this and you will live."

> But wanting to justify himself, he asked Jesus, "And who is my neighbor?"

> Jesus took up the question and said: "A man was going down from Jerusalem to Jericho and fell into the hands of robbers. They stripped him, beat him up, and fled, leaving him half dead. A priest happened to be going down that road. When he saw him, he passed by on the other side. In the same way, a Levite, when he arrived at the place and saw him, passed by on the other side. But a Samaritan, while traveling, came up to him; and when he saw the man, he had compassion. He went over to him and bandaged his wounds, pouring on oil and wine. Then he put him on his own animal,

brought him to an inn, and took care of him. The next day he took out two denarii, gave them to the innkeeper, and said, 'Take care of him; and when I come back I'll reimburse you for whatever extra you spend.'

"Which of these three do you think proved to be a neighbor to the man who fell into the hands of the robbers?"

"The one who showed mercy to him," he said.

Then Jesus told him, "Go and do the same."

- Who today might be like the priest or the Levite?

- What groups of people today might be enemies the way the Jews and the Samaritans were enemies then?

- List the things the Samaritan did for the victim.

- With whom do you identify in the story?

- Have you ever been in need? Who helped you?

- Who is your enemy? Whom are you prejudiced against? If you were lying helpless and wounded in a ditch, would you accept help from this person?

- Would you notice someone in need? Would you help this person?

- According to Jesus' parable, who is your neighbor?

DARE
Which person in the story proved to be a neighbor?

Go and do the same.

CARE
This week make an intentional effort of be aware of strangers in need and find ways to help them.

PRAYER
Lord, make me an instrument of your peace. Where there is hatred, let me sow love; where there is injury, pardon; where there is doubt, faith; where there is despair, hope; where there is darkness, light; where there is sadness, joy. O, Divine Master, grant that I may not so much seek to be consoled as to console; to be understood as to understand; to be loved as to love. For it is in giving that we receive; it is in pardoning that we are pardoned; and it is in dying that we are born to eternal life. Amen.

—St. Francis of Assisi

AWARE

Neighbor—The Bible records a number of directives concerning the treatment of a neighbor but little definition as to what or who a neighbor is. In Exodus the term is first used in a way which crosses ethnic or national bounds. The most important teaching to define a neighbor came from Jesus' answer to the question, "Who is my neighbor?" Jesus responded by giving the parable of the good Samaritan.

Priest—Person in charge of sacrifice and offering at worship places, particularly the tabernacle and temple. Priesthood in the Old Testament primarily involved sacrificing at the altar and worship in the shrine. Other functions were blessing the people, discerning the will of God, and instructing the people in the law of God. This instruction included the application of the laws of cleanness.

Levite—Israel's first priests and temple personnel were drawn from the firstborn of every family in Israel. Later God chose the tribe of Levi to carry out this responsibility for Israel.

The Levites were not given a tribal inheritance in the promised land (God was their inheritance) but were placed in 48 Levitical cities throughout the land. The tithe of the rest of the nation was used to provide for the needs of the Levites. Since the Levites were dependent on the generosity of others, families were encouraged to invite the Levites (as well as widows, strangers, and orphans) to join them in their eating and their celebration of the joyous national feast.

The Levites were consecrated to God and given by God as a gift to Israel in order that they might perform the duties at the tabernacle. During the wilderness journey they were in charge of taking the tabernacle down, transporting it, setting it up, and conducting worship at the tent where God dwelt. During David's reign the Levites had other roles, including judges, craftsmen, musicians, and overseers of the royal treasury. Later the Levites were involved with teaching the people the Word of God.

Samaritan—The name *Samaritans* originally was identified with the Israelites of the Northern Kingdom. When the Assyrians conquered Israel and exiled the Israelites, a "remnant of Israel" remained in the land. Assyrian captives from distant places also settled there. This led to the intermarriage of some, though not all, Jews with Gentiles and to widespread worship of foreign gods. By the time the Jews returned to Jerusalem to rebuild the temple and the walls of Jerusalem, Ezra and Nehemiah refused to let the Samaritans share in the experience. The old antagonism between Israel to the north and Judah to the south intensified the quarrel.

In Jesus' day the relationship between the Jews and the Samaritans was strained. The animosity was so great that the Jews avoided going through Samaria by crossing the Jordan River and traveling on the eastern side of the Jordan. Yet Jesus rebuked His disciples for their hostility to the Samaritans, healed a Samaritan leper, honored a Samaritan for his neighborliness, praised a Samaritan for his gratitude, asked a drink of a Samaritan woman, and preached to the Samaritans. Then in Acts 1:8, Jesus challenged His disciples to witness in Samaria. Philip, a deacon, opened a mission in Samaria.

Sermon Notes / **Love Your Neighbor**

Scripture Text

Main Points

1.

2.

3.

Meaningful Illustrations

Personal Application

36 DAY The Command to Love

We have been commanded to love people.

Today there's no humorous story, no parable, no inspiring profile to set before your eyes. Just reflect on this one phrase. Take it in slowly. Let it sink down into the core of who you are. Hear that truth (and truth it is!) as if you were hearing it for the very first time.

You have been commanded to love people.

You can't talk your way out of that one. You must love. Jesus commanded, "I give you a new commandment: that you should love one another. Just as I have loved you, so you too should love one another" (John 13:34, AMP). The parameter which was wide and inclusive completely disappears when Jesus says, "Love your enemies. Help and give without expecting a return" (Luke 6:35, *The Message*).

He tossed out the old self-preserving, me-first mind-set and called us to be the most passionate, curiously peculiar people that the world has ever known. This is the kind of love that makes a practice out of extreme love. Love goes deeper than appeasing, compromising, and tolerating. It runs beyond treaties, borders, and time limits. This love is a powerful, courageous love. It's putting skin and bones on Christianity. It endures. It hopes. It believes.

Jesus goes on to say:

> You'll never—I promise—regret it. Live out this God-created identity the way our Father lives toward us, generously and graciously, even when we're at our worst (Luke 6:35, *The Message*).

In other words, don't just practice this radical mission of love on the nice days when the car works, the garbage has been taken out, and your kids are sweet and admirable. Don't just camp out in the wilderness of love. (And it is wilderness—uncharted, unlimited, and adventurous!) Build your home there.

DARE

Who is one difficult person in your life you can bless (and perhaps even startle) with God's love? Just do it.

No Exclusions

Jesus came to earth with no exclusions. He did not come only for the Jews of the Middle East. Nor did He come as a white man's Messiah. He came for slaves who toiled under oppression, for hate-driven extremists. He came into the Far East through missionaries and martyrs. He came to Native Americans, Russians, and Scandinavians. His Spirit has challenged every border, every tongue, and every society. His truth roams freely, seeking whom He may redeem. He came for the sinners, the rebels, and the vagabonds.

The Lord sees the spiritually emaciated world, and His invitation hasn't changed, Is anyone thirsty? Come and drink—even if you have no money! Come, take your choice of wine or milk—it's all free! Why spend your money on food that does not give you strength? Why pay for food that does you no good? Listen, and I will tell you where to get food that is good for the soul! (Isa. 55:1-2, NLT).

Who is to embody the Greatest Commandment? We are. We aren't to harass, condemn, or shame people into relationship with God. Jesus told the upper echelon of temple-goers:

How terrible it will be for you teachers of religious law and you Pharisees. Hypocrites! You are like whitewashed tombs—beautiful on the outside but filled on the inside with dead people's bones and all sorts of impurity (Matt. 23:27, NLT).

Most of the religious people never got it. They were so caught up in the guilt business that they drove right past the glory of grace. Their tribe is increasing even today. They still choose philosophy over ministry. They are more concerned about why bad things happen than how good things are born from bad. They major on the minors. They find comfort in parameters. They gossip about and critique one another, trying to explain away God's work and formulate the newest program. They are more comfortable with the trappings of their religion than with the manifestation of God's glory.

Christ is in your corner. He is your Friend, not the prosecuting attorney. Even though you've been given an incredible task, you can rely on Him. If you speak the truth and no one accepts it. If you run through the fire and you are left without a friend. If you are far from the applause of your peers and your family. If no one sees a thing you do for Christ. It doesn't matter. You don't have to obsess over how you look, what you accomplish, where you are sent. "If God is for us, who can be against us?" (Rom. 8:31, NIV).

PRAYER

Lord, I confess the tendency of my old nature to connect only with people who are like me. I confess my spiritual nearsightedness. I need You to manifest Yourself in my everyday life. Give me the courage to love beyond reason.

38 DAY Loving People Over Things

God says to love the people around you. No matter who they may be, they are important to Him.

Our world values people who help us do what we want to do and be who we want to be. That's the opposite of God's plan. God's plan says don't let your earthly goods interfere with loving the people around you.

This value is illustrated in the Gospel of Luke. Jesus encountered the best and brightest young man in town. Give him credit. Spiritual things interested him. He wanted to be a kingdom man, so he asked Jesus what his next step should be. What could he do? Jesus handed him the truth. It stopped him in his tracks.

> Go and sell everything you have and give the proceeds to people who need it more than you. Then come and follow me (see Luke 18:22).

People first.
Sadly, the rich man walked away from an eternity of contentment.

> This was the last thing the official expected to hear. He was very rich and became terribly sad. He was holding on tight to a lot of things and not about to let them go (Luke 18:23, *The Message*).

Jesus didn't require this of everyone who came to Him, but He knew the wall of wealth that kept this man from loving his neighbor as he loved himself. Whenever we value stuff over people, we lose. Whenever we value position more than people, we fail. Whenever we value programs more than people, we've lost a vision for what Christian ministry is all about.

What is it that's stuck in your house, or in your mind, or in your nest egg, or on your computer that is blocking your ability to love people? Forget the wealth calculators and retirement planning tools! The true measure of wealth is found in the number of people you've loved into a relationship with Jesus. It's impossible to pick up the cross and follow Jesus if your hands are already full.

DARE
Experience a rich young ruler moment right now. What is it that is in your hand or on your heart which is interfering with the important task of loving people with a godly love? What are you going to do about it?

The Victim

The world doesn't care about words that aren't backed up by love.

A certain man was going down from a casino to a bar, when he fell into the hands of mobsters. They stripped him of his clothes, beat him, and left him half dead.

A familiar face appeared on the other side of the road, a man from the church he attended before his addictions took over. "Is that you? Trouble again, huh? What was it this time? A gambling debt? Are you drunk? Did you think that I would actually help you after all you've put your family through? Think about all the sacrifices people have made on your behalf. Maybe this is what you deserve. I'm on to you. You have a fatal flaw. You never have amounted to anything, and you never will. Well, I'm late for a prayer meeting." And he passed by on the other side.

Soon a woman from the church library walked over. "I'm glad you're still here. I saw you from the road and went back to the church. I picked up a few books for you to borrow. You'll need to return them. Let's see, here's *Pulling Yourself Up by Your Bootstraps* and *I'm Not OK, You're Not OK, but That's OK*. And I've got *Seven Habits of Well-Adjusted People* and *When You Feel Drop-Kicked by Life*. Here's a book you'll find helpful: *Who Moved My First-Aid Kit?* Take your time. Try not to get blood on the covers. Some are first editions." She dropped the book bag at his feet and walked away.

Another man hesitantly came by a few minutes later and yelled to him from the opposite side of the road. "Hi over there. Sorry. I just knew I had to do something, but I get kind of queasy when I see blood. Don't worry. I'm just a concerned citizen. I'm going to throw something over to you," he yelled. "Do not be alarmed! Stay calm."

The man pulled out a box and threw it over to him. It miraculously landed beside him.

"What's this?" the outcast asked.

"Moist towelettes! They are refreshing with a mild scent of lemon. Keep the box. I hope you feel better now." And the squeamish man passed on the other side of the road.

The old adage still rings true. "People will not care how much you know until they know how much you care."

Your neighbors aren't looking for someone to remind them about how terrible they are. They aren't looking for information or quick fixes. They are looking for Jesus, even if they don't say the word *Jesus*. Their hearts are seeking Him. They might not say His name, but they yearn for what He is—grace, truth, and love.

CARE

Commit today to express care to someone who is walking through a valley of grief, hurt, or disillusionment.

40 DAY Who Are You?

What's your name? When your neighbors see you, whom do they see?

Addict? Friend? Brother? Helper? Writer? Saint? Cynic? Dreamer? Disillusioned? Sorrowful one? Motivator? Fan? Outcast? Desperate one? Legalist?

Labels are convenient. We can hide behind them. Some lower expectations; others heighten them. Some people try to lose their labels; others depend on them. But they stick like clothes with static cling. Labels define us. Some give us authority—like diplomas, badges, and uniforms. Others accuse us—like warrants, petitions, and anonymous letters.

Who are you? Can you live up to your label? Can you overcome your label? In the end, the only label that really matters will be the one you receive from a holy God and His perfect Son. He calls you. He knows you. He names you. When you find your hope in Him, the labels melt, and you are given a new name.

> I no longer call you servants, because a servant does not know his master's business. Instead, I have called you friends, for everything that I learned from my Father I have made known to you (John 15:15, NIV).

"'Then all the nations will call you blessed, for yours will be a delightful land,' says the LORD Almighty" (Mal. 3:12, NIV). "And the LORD said to Moses, 'I will do the very thing you have asked, because I am pleased with you and I know you by name'" (Ex. 33:17, NIV).

When you enter into relationship with Jesus, He gives you an eternal name. As a member of His family, you have a new name, and you have the power that comes through you but not from you. You are . . .

- The salt of the earth (Matt. 5:13)
- The light of the world (Matt. 5:14)
- The children of God (John 1:12)
- The bride of Christ (John 3:29)
- Branches of the one true Vine (John 15:5)
- Witnesses for Jesus (Acts 1:8)
- Containers of God's glory (2 Cor. 4:5-7)
- Ambassadors for Christ (2 Cor. 5:20)
- Soldiers of the Lord (Eph. 6:10-11)
- Partakers of His grace (Phil. 1:7)
- A holy nation (1 Pet. 2:9)
- Overcomers (1 John 4:4)

These are the labels you are given that will never be destroyed! Do you understand what that means? Do you savor this adventure? Do you rise victorious in the heat of the battle? He whispers, "Fear not. You are My child. I call you by name."

DECLARE

Spend some time today reading and meditating on Isaiah 45:2-3, Isaiah 62:4. What names were you given by others? What new name is God giving you as we conclude this 40-day experience?

Loving God, Loving Others

There is one God, and He wants you first to love Him with all you are and have and then to love others as much as you love yourself.

In the early morning hours of February 3, 1943, the American troop ship *Dorchester,* en route to a top secret radar installation in Greenland, was torpedoed by a German submarine. Four Army chaplains were on board that ship.

Most of the passengers aboard the *Dorchester* were asleep when the German sub was first detected. Awakened from their sleep, the men ran to battle stations, weathering the icy seas. Twice they were awakened; twice there were false alarms. Each time fewer men arrived on deck wearing a life jacket. The third time the men were awakened, not by an alarm, but by the ear-splitting sound and the rattling concussion that could only mean the ship had been hit by a torpedo.

Men staggered to the deck, many without their life jackets. Three lifeboats had been destroyed in the blast. When crews tried to launch life boats, they found them encased in a heavy layer of ice. The first lifeboat to hit the water capsized, hurling the men into 36°F water. Finally, one lifeboat launched successfully.

The men remaining on deck began to panic as they realized the ship was sinking. A frantic search ensued for life jackets. Soon all those on deck were gone, and the men could no longer go below deck to find more.

The chaplains were working to help the men into lifeboats and life jackets. Some men without jackets began to cry, realizing that death was near. With no thought for self and no collaboration, first one chaplain and then another removed his life jacket and gave it to a soldier. As the ship went down—just 20 minutes after being hit, those afloat in boats and life jackets saw the four chaplains, standing arm in arm on the deck of the ship, slowly sink beneath the waves.

SHARE

Of the three love relationship noted in the Greatest Commandment—God, self, others—which is strongest for you? weakest?

DECLARE

1. **Read Mark 12:28-34:**

> One of the scribes approached. When he heard them debating and saw that Jesus answered them well, he asked Him, "Which commandment is the most important of all?"

"This is the most important," Jesus answered:

Hear, O Israel! The Lord our God is one Lord. And you shall love the Lord your God with all your heart, with all your soul, with all your mind, and with all your strength.

"The second is: You shall love your neighbor as yourself. There is no other commandment greater than these."

Then the scribe said to Him, "Well said, Teacher! You have spoken in truth that He is one, and there is no one else except Him. And to love Him with all the heart, with all the understanding, and with all the strength, and to love one's neighbor as oneself, is far more important than all the burnt offerings and sacrifices."

When Jesus saw that he answered intelligently, He said to him, "You are not far from the kingdom of God." And no one dared to question Him any longer.

• When the man restated the words Jesus had spoken, what did he change or add?

• Jesus said the man had answered _____.

• His restatement showed understanding. What is the difference between understanding a truth and applying it?

- Jesus said the man was not far from the _____. How close are you?

- What are the gaps in your understanding? in your applying?

2. **Read Deuteronomy 6:4-9:**

   Hear, O Israel: The LORD our God, the LORD is one. Love the LORD your God with all your heart and with all your soul and with all your strength. These commandments that I give you today are to be upon your hearts. Impress them on your children. Talk about them when you sit at home and when you walk along the road, when you lie down and when you get up. Tie them as symbols on your hands and bind them on your foreheads. Write them on the doorframes of your houses and on your gates (NIV).

- List the ways the Hebrew people were to recall and teach and apply the Scripture.

- List similar ways we can apply the Greatest Commandment today.

DARE

Have you made a decision to follow Christ?

If you are a Christian, is He your one and only God? Do you love Him completely?

CARE

How can you communicate God's love and your love to unbelievers? friends and family? enemies?

PRAYER

Paul prayed for his friends at Ephesus. This is our prayer for you.

For this reason I bow my knees before the Father from whom every family in heaven and on earth is named. I pray that He may grant you, according to the riches of His glory, to be strengthened with power through His Spirit in the inner man, and that the Messiah may dwell in your hearts through faith. I pray that you, being rooted and firmly established in love, may be able to comprehend with all the saints what is the breadth and width, height and depth, and to know the Messiah's love that surpasses knowledge, so you may be filled with all the fullness of God. Now to Him who is able to do above and beyond all that we ask or think—according to the power that works in you—to Him be glory in the church and in Christ Jesus to all generations, forever and ever. Amen (Eph. 3:14-21).

AWARE

Parables—Stories, especially those of Jesus, told to provide a vision of life, especially life in God's kingdom. *Parable* means "a putting alongside for purposes of comparison and new understanding." Parables use word pictures such as metaphors or similes and frequently extend them into a brief story to make a point or disclosure. A parable may convey images and implications, but it has only one main point established by a basic comparison or internal juxtaposition. Parable is the basic device Jesus used in His teaching. A parable, as opposed to an allegory, establishes a basic, single comparison and aids interpretation.

Jesus could turn people's ears into eyes with a word picture. He spoke simple parables that represent a picture elaborated into a story, often using images common to His audience. These extended pictures portray a general situation growing out of a typical experience and appealing to common sense. A narrative parable is a dramatic story composed of one or more scenes drawn from daily life, yet focused on an unusual decisive circumstance.

Jesus intended to involve His hearers, and so He constructed many parables; each parable amounts to one big question for the hearer/reader. Questions within a parable often define a dilemma. Direct discourse is also immensely important in many of the parables because it brings the stories to life. Through human conversation the parable often makes its point, especially in the last speech. The parables of Jesus were evangelistic because they sought to stimulate and change people's lives. They invited the audience to repent and believe. They were intended to awaken faith.

Kingdom of God—God's kingly rule or sovereignty. In the New Testament the fullest revelation of God's divine rule is in the person of Jesus Christ. Jesus preached that God's kingdom was at hand. His miracles, preaching, forgiving sins, and resurrection are an in-breaking of God's sovereign rule in this dark, evil age.

God's kingdom was manifested in the church. Jesus commissioned the making of disciples on the basis of His kingly authority. God's kingdom may be understood in terms of "reign or realm." Reign conveys the fact that God exerts His divine authority over His subjects/kingdom. Realm suggests location, and God's realm is universal. God's reign extends over all things. He is universally sovereign over the nations, humankind, the angels, the dominion of darkness and its inhabitants, and even the cosmos, individual believers, and the church.

The kingdom of God is the work of God, not produced by human ingenuity. God brought it into the world through Christ, and it presently works through the church. The church preaches the kingdom of God and anticipates the eventual consummation.

The kingdom of God means the reign of God in the lives of His people, enabling them to serve Him wholeheartedly. The kingdom of God, in its simplest form, is the reign of Jesus Christ as Lord and King in our lives.

Sermon Notes / **Loving God, Loving Others**

Scripture Text

Main Points
1.

2.

3.

Meaningful Illustrations

Personal Application

Bibliography

Brand, Chad, Charles Draper, and Archie England, general editors; Steve Bond and E. Ray Clendenen, associate editors; Trent C. Butler, general editor, *Holman Bible Dictionary;* Bill Latta, biblical reconstructions. *Holman Illustrated Bible Dictionary.* Nashville: Broadman & Holman, 2003. Used in "Aware" sections of small-group sessions.

Brooks, James A. *Mark. Vol. 23 of The New American Commentary.* Nashville: Broadman Press, 1991.

Carlisle, Paul. *With All My Heart: God's Design for Emotional Wellness.* Nashville: LifeWay Press, 2000.

Coleman, Lyman, ed. *Serendipity Bible for Groups,* 4th ed. Grand Rapids: Serendipity House, 1988.

Edgemon, Roy, and Barry Sneed. *Jesus by Heart: God Can Transform You to Be like Jesus.* Nashville: LifeWay Press, 1999.

Hunt, T. W., and Claude V. King. *The Mind of Christ.* Nashville: LifeWay Press, 1994.

Lucado, Max *In the Grip of Grace.* Dallas: Word Publishing, 1996.

McQuilkin, Robertson. *Life in the Spirit.* Nashville: LifeWay Press, 1997.

Mims, Gene. *The Kingdom Focused Church.* Nashville: Broadman & Holman, 2003.

Moore, Beth. *Jesus the One and Only.* Nashville: Broadman & Holman, 2002.

Porowski, James P. *With All My Mind: God's Design for Mental Wellness.* Nashville: LifeWay Press, 2002.

Tullos, Matt. *Aha Moments: 200 Short Dramatic Scripts for Worship.* Nashville: Church Street Press, 2002.

Tullos, Matt. *Actors Not Included: 303 Scripts for Church Drama.* CD-Rom. Nashville: LifeWay Press, 1999.

Tullos, Matt and Darlene Tullos. *And Now You Know the Rest of His Glory.* Hermitage: Wordspring Creative Ministries, 2001.

Wales, Ken, and David Poling. *Sea of Glory.* Nashville: Broadman & Holman, 2001.

Wilkes, Gene. *With All My Soul: God's Design for Spiritual Wellness.* Nashville: LifeWay Press, 2001.

CHRISTIAN GROWTH STUDY PLAN

In the **Christian Growth Study Plan (formerly Church Study Course),** this book *Extreme Love: The Greatest Commandment* is a resource for course credit in the subject area Personal Life of the Christian Growth category of plans. To receive credit, read the book, complete the learning activities, show your work to your pastor, a staff member or church leader, then complete the following information. This page may be duplicated. Send the completed page to:

**Christian Growth Study Plan
One LifeWay Plaza, Nashville, TN 37234-0117
FAX: (615)251-5067 • E-mail: *cgspnet@lifeway.com***
For information about the Christian Growth Study Plan, refer to the Christian Growth Study Plan Catalog. It is located online at *www.lifeway.com/cgsp*. If you do not have access to the Internet, contact the Christian Growth Study Plan office (1.800.968.5519) for the specific plan you need for your ministry.

EXTREME LOVE: THE GREATEST COMMANDMENT
COURSE NUMBER: CG-1026

PARTICIPANT INFORMATION

Social Security Number (USA ONLY-optional)	Personal CGSP Number*	Date of Birth (MONTH, DAY, YEAR)

Name (First, Middle, Last)		Home Phone

Address (Street, Route, or P.O. Box)	City, State, or Province	Zip/Postal Code

Please check appropriate box: ❑ Resource purchased by self ❑ Resource purchased by church ❑ Other

CHURCH INFORMATION

Church Name

Address (Street, Route, or P.O. Box)	City, State, or Province	Zip/Postal Code

CHANGE REQUEST ONLY

☐ Former Name		

☐ Former Address	City, State, or Province	Zip/Postal Code

☐ Former Church	City, State, or Province	Zip/Postal Code

Signature of Pastor, Conference Leader, or Other Church Leader	Date

*New participants are requested but not required to give SS# and date of birth. Existing participants, please give CGSP# when using SS# for the first time. Thereafter, only one ID# is required. **Mail to:** Christian Growth Study Plan, One LifeWay Plaza, Nashville, TN 37234-0117. Fax: (615)251-5067.

Rev. 3-03

Ideas for Leading Small-Group Sessions

SESSION CHARACTERISTICS

Small-group sessions in this 40-day experience are designed with these characteristics:

Forty-day experience sessions are planned to be open to anyone who wants to participate. Questions and content assume that both Christians and seekers, church members and potential members, will participate together in these sessions.

Forty-day experience sessions are insight driven. Most Bible study groups are content driven: participants learn from reading and hearing teacher-led, content-based information; the teacher-leader of a session provides more information than the learner generally has in learner resources. Small-group sessions in this resource are insight driven. Insights of all participants should be encouraged. Participants in the group learn from one another.

Forty-day experience sessions are designed so the leader can be a member of the group, and any group member can be the leader. Because the small-group process in this resource does not depend on someone to prepare and share information, little advance preparation is needed. The leader is a guide more than a teacher.

THE LEADER'S ROLE

1. *To get to know members of the small group*—Sessions tend to build in intimacy throughout the 40 days. Questions become a bit more personal throughout the sessions. The leader's knowledge of and sensitivity to group members will ensure that all members are comfortable in the sessions. For example, if the group is open and all members share freely with one another, more time may be spent on sharing questions. On the other hand, if the group members share less freely and a question seems more personal, members may be encouraged to write a response without sharing it, or the leader may spend only a short time processing an answer aloud, with a few volunteers verbalizing their responses.

2. *To encourage everyone to participate*—The quietest member may have the deepest insights but share them only with encouragement or when everyone else has spoken. On the other hand, if some members tend to dominate the sessions, the leader may need to interrupt politely and say, "Thanks so much for your contribution. Let's hear from some of the others."

3. *To be comfortable with silence*—Allow participants time to think. Encourage others to speak. The leader's responsibility is not to step in and share insights or content as much as it is to create a comfortable environment for all to participate.

4. *To affirm all learners*—Because the content is insight driven, all members should be affirmed when they respond. When members do not see a passage of Scripture the same way, they can learn from one another.
5. *To prepare brief commentary about a few points in the session*—The purpose of this commentary should be to enhance discussion rather than to control the direction of the group or to provide a lecture.
6. *To plan the flow of the session so that all parts are covered*—Each session has seven parts. The parts of the session generally follow the same sequence, but sometimes the first two are reversed.

   Beginning narrative—The first part is a narrative that captures the application of the session. The story may be fiction, a Scripture passage, a biblical paraphrase, or vignettes from contemporary life. The leader may tell the story, enlist someone else in advance to tell the story or present it dramatically, invite someone in class to read it aloud, or invite participants to read it silently.

 Share uses questions to help group members interact with and learn about one another. These questions are intended to be ice breakers, nonthreatening ways to encourage members to speak freely during the sessions. They are not intended to launch discussions of intimate details of members' lives. Nor are they intended to become the focus of the session. The leader will need to manage the time well so that not too much of the session is spent on this introductory element.

This time is important, however. Questions set the stage for discussions throughout the session and are always related to the focus of the session.

 Declare contains questions that guide group members to examine the Bible verses. This is the heart of the Bible study and where you will spend most of your time.

   The leader will have opportunities in this section to guide the study and provide additional information, but this is not meant to be a lecture. Participants should learn through personal insights of biblical truths. Everyone should be encouraged to share.

Although persons with knowledge of the Bible are helpful resources, each person's insight is important. Allow the Bible to speak to individuals rather than spending all the time imparting information about the Scripture passages being studied.

Dare challenges group members to apply the Bible verses to their lives. The questions in this section encourage group members to make important spiritual commitments.

Depending on the group's comfort level in talking freely, you may spent some time discussing these, ask only a few to volunteer a response, or invite members to respond privately by writing in their own books.

Care suggests ways for group members to show love and concern for one another and for people outside their small group. During some sessions you may want to explore options for ways to respond. The group may also want to consider a group project that relates to a special need or a church ministry.

Prayer directs participants to communicate with God about a need revealed in this session. Explore different ways of praying during these weeks—silent prayers, sentence prayers, written prayers, prayer journals, guided prayers.

Aware contains helpful information to assist group members in understanding the meaning of the Scripture. A few key elements from the Scripture passages being studied each week have been selected to provide background information that may be helpful for you to share during the session.

How to Become a Christian

Some people think a personal relationship with God is something only theologians can comprehend. Actually, God's plan of salvation is simple enough for everyone to understand. Here are the ABCs of salvation.

Admit

Admit to God that you are a sinner. All persons need salvation. Each of us has a problem the Bible calls sin. Sin is a refusal to acknowledge God's authority over our lives. Everyone who does not live a life of perfect obedience to the Lord is guilty to sin. "For all have sinned and fall short of the glory of God" (Rom. 3:23). Since none of us is perfect, all of us are sinners (Rom. 3:10-18). The result of sin is spiritual death (Rom. 6:23). Spiritual death means eternal separation from God. By God's perfect standard we are guilty of sin and therefore subject tot he punishment for sin, which is separation from God. Admitting that you are a sinner and separated from God is the first step of repentance, which is turning from sin and self and turning toward God.

Believe

Believe in Jesus Christ as God's Son and receive Jesus' gift of forgiveness from sin. God loves each of u. God offers us salvation. Although we have done nothing to deserve His love and salvation. God wants to save us. In the death of Jesus on the cross, God provided salvation for all who would repent of their sins and believe in Jesus. "For God loved the world in this way: He gave His One and Only Son, so that everyone who believes in Him will not perish but have eternal life" (John 3:16).

Confess

Confess your faith in Jesus Christ as Savior and Lord to others. After you have received Jesus Christ into your life, share your decision with another person. Tell your pastor or a Christian friend about your decision. Following Christ's example, ask for baptism by immersion in your local church as a public expression of your faith. "If you confess with your mouth, 'Jesus is Lord,' and believe in your heart that God raised Him from the dead, you will be saved. With the heart one believes, resulting in righteousness, and with the mouth one confesses, resulting in salvation" (Rom. 10:9-10).